ENDORSEMENTS

"Spending time in nature can be a great way for parents and children to connect. Often, however, today's parents feel unsure about how to guide their children's time in nature so that it is meaningful and leads to a greater understanding and appreciation of the natural world. Luckily, Asia Citro's new book *A Little Bit of Dirt* will guide, inspire, and encourage you to spend more time in nature as a family. This resourceful book contains many exciting project ideas designed to engage children and their parents while providing valuable lessons about nature and its processes. The Extensions ideas in each chapter are a wonderful way to scaffold the learning and increase children's problem solving skills through open-ended questions."

—Erin Kenny
Director of Cedarsong Nature School
Author of *Forest Kindergartens: The Cedarsong Way*

"Asia Citro's newest book *A Little Bit of Dirt* hits the right mark for giving parents, kids, and families simple and tangible ways for connecting with nature—just beyond the doorstep. Enticing photographs accompany fun, interactive exercises. An inspiring addition to the Nature Activity section of your bookshelf."

—Clare Walker Leslie
Author of *The Nature Connection* and *Keeping a Nature Journal*

"In 10 years, your kids probably aren't going to remember the video game or iPhone app they were playing, but I guarantee you they'll remember digging in the dirt with the activities from this wonderful book. Get out there and get your hands dirty with them!"

—Stacy Tornio
Author of *The Kids' Outdoor Adventure Book* and *Project Garden*

"This clearly designed book is full of easy-to-follow, achievable activities, inviting children to run outside, be creative, and discover the magic of the wild world."

—Jo Schofield and Fiona Danks
Authors of *The Stick Book* and seven other *Going Wild* books

"Asia Citro's book, *A Little Bit of Dirt*, inspires my imagination! Seriously. I can't wait to make dandelion bubbles with the neighborhood kids! Kids love to be active, to be outdoors, to be creative. Asia's book incorporates all of this and more. I highly recommend that all kids discover the outdoors through Asia's creative activities, including my favorites: Nature Boats, Texture Garden, and Nature Weaving. Kids will learn to treasure and care for their outdoor environment while using imagination and creativity."

—MaryAnn F. Kohl
Bestselling author of over 20 children's art books

"*A Little Bit of Dirt* recognizes, quite rightly, that nature is the perfect classroom for kids. Asia's book is the ideal resource for anyone wanting to teach children important lessons through play, exploration... and getting just a little bit muddy!"

—Dawn Isaac
Author of *101 Things for Kids To Do Outside*,
101 Things for Kids To Do On A Rainy Day, and *Garden Crafts for Children*

"With inviting photographs and activities that dazzle, Asia Citro's *A Little Bit of Dirt* is a treasure trove of ideas to inspire families to get outside and delight in nature. From building and listening to Rain Drums to creating a Texture Garden, Earthworm Towers, Sun Prints, and Sticky Nature Bracelets, this book is chock full of fresh ideas for getting kids to wonder about the hows, the whys, and the what's that nature has to offer. This book is going in my library and when it does, more than likely it will be well-worn and covered with a little bit of dirt!"

—Lynn Brunelle
Author of *Camp Out! The Ultimate Kids' Guide* and *Pop Bottle Science*

"Helping a child forge deep connections with nature is among the most powerful and lasting gifts that any of us can give. An essential ingredient on this journey is abundant, hands-on experiences in nearby nature. In this delightful book, Asia Citro offers up a smorgasbord of engaging activities, many of them marrying art and science as a catalyst to wonder. With *A Little Bit of Dirt* in your hands, you're well on your way to becoming a star nature mentor for the kids in your life!"

—Scott D. Sampson
Host of the hit PBS KIDS series *Dinosaur Train*, and author of *How to Raise a Wild Child*

A Little Bit of Dirt

55+ Science and Art Activities to Reconnect Children with Nature

Asia Citro, MEd

author of *150+ Screen-Free Activities for Kids*

THE INNOVATION PRESS

Published by
The Innovation Press
P.O. Box 2584, Woodinville, WA 98072-2584. U.S.A.
www.theinnovationpress.com

ISBN 978-1-943147-04-5

Printed and bound in China.
Production Date: 07/2016
Batch Number: 67297-0
Plant Location: Everbest

10 9 8 7 6 5 4 3

Many of the designations used by manufacturers and sellers to distinguish their products are claimed as trademarks. Where those designations appear in this book and The Innovation Press was aware of a trademark claim, the designations have been printed with initial capital letters.

All of the activities in this book are intended to be performed under adult supervision. Appropriate and reasonable caution is recommended when activities call for any objects that could be of risk, such as hot glue, sharp scissors, or small objects that could present a choking hazard. If you are unsure of the safety or age appropriateness of an activity, please contact your child's doctor for guidance. The recommendations in the activities in this book cannot replace common sense and sound judgment. Observe safety and caution at all times. The author and publisher disclaim liability for any damage, mishap, or injury that may occur from engaging in the activities described in this book.

Photography by Asia Citro.
Lunchbox font by Kimmy Design.
Frente font by Frente.
Cover design by Kerry Ellis.

To Goose and Bubba, always.

Acknowledgments

First, a big thank-you to my family for their support. I couldn't have written and photographed this book without the help and cooperation of my kids and the child care provided by my husband and mom.

Thank you to Betsy Adams for helping me double-check my scientific accuracy and to Patricia Pyle for introducing me to the wonderful world of environmental education. Thank you to my mom, my husband, and Stephanie Haass for all of your help poring over the introduction and helping me get it right! Thank you to my talented and patient graphic designer, Kerry Ellis, for bringing my vision for the book to life. Thank you to my editor, Cynthia Reeh, for helping me with all the finishing touches. And thank you to my friends for donating your children for photo shoots of the activities!

Thank you to all of our *Fun at Home with Kids* blog readers, our *150+ Screen-Free Activities for Kids* book readers, and *The Curious Kid's Science Book* readers for your lovely comments, messages, and photos. We love hearing from you and your support means the world to us!

Thank you to Discount School Supply and Astrobrights for providing some of the materials in this book.

Thank you to Chelsey Marashian (BuggyandBuddy.com), Kirstin Therese (Craftiments.com), Deborah Stewart (TeachPreschool.org), Ann Harmon Harquail (MyNearestandDearest.com), Louise McMullen (MessyLittleMonster.com), Edith Sisson (Nature with Children of all Ages), Project Learning Tree (plt.org), Project WET Foundation (projectwet.org), and The Inspired Treehouse (theinspiredtreehouse.com) for inspiring an activity in the book with your work.

Table of Contents

Introduction

The rain is falling fast and hard. Our rain drums sit on the kitchen counter, looking like bright rainbows of color waiting to brighten an otherwise dreary fall day. We have to know—what beat will the rain play for us this morning? We suit up. Rain jackets and boots on with drums piled in our arms, we head out giggling into the downpour. Full of excitement, we set out our rain drums and huddle together to enjoy the beautiful songs nature is making for us on this wet, gray day.

It's easiest to imagine outdoor play on a sunny, warm day, maybe even on a beach with waves crashing and warm sand between your toes, but outdoor play is important for kids year-round. Study after study has shown that regularly spending time in nature fosters healthy, happy, centered kids. The findings are so convincing that some doctors and pediatricians even write prescriptions

> "When you're sitting in front of a screen, you're not using all of your senses at the same time. Nowhere than in nature do kids use their senses in such a stimulated way."
> –RICHARD LOUV

for their patients to spend time in nature! In this book I hope you find inspiration to get outside with your family, strengthen your connection with and understanding of nature, and experience the benefits of regular outdoor time.

As our world becomes more complicated, structured, and technological, we get fewer simple, slow, and calm moments in our days. With school, extracurricular activities, and the lure of our technological devices, it's easy for outdoor play to fall by the wayside. But outdoor play is a needed balance to our busy modern days. Rather than just providing visual stimulation, as many of our indoor activities tend to do, outdoor play activates all the senses. Outdoor terrain is uneven, which challenges and develops our children's motor skills in ways that manufactured surfaces can't. Outdoor environments provide larger spaces for our children to run, skip, and climb—to keep their hearts and muscles strong. Time spent in nature is important to the development of healthy children.

Not only is spending time outdoors important to the well-being and growth of our children, but it's also vital to nature. As the world population grows, development continues to encroach on and affect what wild spaces we have left. Children need personal experiences with the natural world before they can begin to value and cherish it. Only then will they be motivated to take the steps necessary to conserve our precious resources as adults. In this sense, making time to acquaint your children with nature now is an investment in the future—for all of us.

"What is the extinction of a Condor to a child who has never seen a wren?"
–ROBERT MICHAEL PYLE

However, time spent with nature doesn't have to be perfect to be valuable. I think we'd all enjoy making art in a spring meadow filled with flowers, but for many of us this is just not possible. Even if you do the Pounding Art activity with store-bought flowers in a high-rise apartment surrounded by snow, your children can still experience the awe of the vibrant colors of the flower transfer, the papery-thin smooth texture of the petals, and the delicate scent released into the air. You can still make important connections to nature even if you don't have regular access to wild spaces.

Unstructured play in nature is ideal, but sometimes I find that my kids—and I—need a little extra motivation to get outside. To that end, the pages of this book contain more than 55 of our favorite nature activities, designed to engage the senses, imagination, and minds of all ages. Take it from me—you don't have to be a child to enjoy wrapping twigs or blowing dandelion bubbles! So get outside, get a little wet, get a little dirty, and make wonderful memories as you experience the beauty of the natural world together.

A Note on Collecting Natural Objects

In this book you will collect a variety of natural objects for the activities. Natural objects are any product or physical matter that comes from plants, animals, or the ground. My hope is that you can collect natural objects from a yard, garden, or park that belongs to you or someone you know. If not, please take care with how you collect these objects—city, state, and national parks have laws to protect natural materials. However, we've found that most places are happy to allow children to collect a few small objects if you ask permission first.

As a general rule, first look on the ground when collecting objects (even from your own yard). If you'd like to collect flowers or leaves from a living plant, try to collect from different places on the plant or from different plants of the same type, so that you aren't stripping one plant of most of its flowers or leaves.

Please also familiarize yourself with anything that is poisonous or can cause itching or stinging so you know to avoid touching them. Many creatures like to eat plants, so plants have to keep themselves safe—but sometimes the ways they keep themselves safe give us a case of the itches!

Framed Nature Art

Decorate the windows of your home with beautiful natural art! In addition to highlighting the beauty of nature, Framed Nature Art is also an interesting experiment—what objects stay the same over time? Which lose their color? As natural materials change by season, this is a fun activity to revisit over time. Can you create art pieces that represent each season?

MATERIALS

☐ Frame from thrift store or old frame you're no longer using

☐ Natural objects   ☐ Glue

☐ Suction cups   ☐ Hot glue

DIRECTIONS

1. Place the frame facedown and remove any paper and backing from the glass/plastic.

2. Add natural objects. For best results, choose objects that lay flat or almost flat against the glass front of the frame.

3. Once you arrange the natural objects as you wish, add enough glue to cover the glass and added objects. For the most permanent artwork, I recommend using Elmer's Glue All rather than a washable glue, but either will work.

4. Allow the artwork to dry for several days. In some cases, depending on how dry and warm the air is, how much glue you've added, and how much moisture the natural objects release, it may take weeks for your artwork to completely dry.

5. Once the artwork is completely dry, lay the frame facedown. Ask an adult to line the back edge of the frame with suction cups and then use a hot glue gun (or, alternately, super glue) to permanently attach the suction cups to the back edge of the frame.

6. Ask an adult to carefully place the artwork in a window (please test that the suction cups are strong enough).

7. Make observations about the materials—which kept their color? Which changed color? Which lost their color? What types of objects look the same? Which look different? Why do you think this is?

Native Plants

Native plants are an important part of any environment. With so many invasive plants and so much landscaping, it's often hard to know what your city looked like before people were around. Invasive plants are plants that aren't supposed to be in an environment, but people plant them (often by accident) and they grow out of control. Invasive plants often take space, sunlight, and nutrients from native species, which makes it harder to find native plants in spaces that are overrun by invasive plants. A healthy natural space usually has a variety of plants that share sunlight and nutrients; when invasive plants come in, they tend to take over everything. Native plants are the plants that are supposed to grow where you live. Before cities and roads and houses, native plants grew all around your city. They are important to the wildlife in your area. Native plants serve as shelter and food for local animals and they play a role in keeping your local water healthy and clean.

For this activity your job is to learn how to identify five native species and to learn one interesting fact about each one. You might need to do a little digging on the internet or ask a local gardening or environmental club to figure out the most common native species to your area. Once you've learned about them, spread the knowledge by teaching others about local native plants!

MATERIALS

☐ Internet search ☐ Camera ☐ Local plant handbook, or local gardening club or store

We wanted to share five of our local native plants with you—if you live in the Pacific Northwest, you might have most (or even all) of these in your neighborhood!

DOUGLAS FIR TREE

One of our favorite things about this tree is the pinecones because of a local myth we heard. In the photo, you'll see a little "mouse" hiding in the pinecone where my daughter is pointing. The mouse tail sticks out and you can see one little mouse ear on each side of the tail. The myth goes like this: Long ago there was a horrible fire in the forest and the forest mice were terribly scared. They decided to climb up the tallest trees in the forest (Douglas firs are the tallest trees in Washington State) and hide inside the pinecones of the giant tree. And to this day, you can still see them hiding in the pinecones with just the tips of their ears and tails showing.

SWORD FERN

Sword ferns are special because of the spore pockets on the back of their leaves. If you ever get stung by stinging nettle (another local native plant), you can rub the brown sori (spore pockets) of the sword fern where you were stung and it will help you feel better.

WESTERN RED CEDAR

The western red cedar was known as the "tree of life" by the native people in our area. They used it to make everything from longhouses to canoes to even clothes! The wood is resistant to mold and insects, making it perfect for long-lasting houses and boats. The bark is very unusual—it's long and bendy so it almost feels like cloth. We also love this tree because it smells wonderful.

SALMONBERRY

We have a lot of native berries where we live—some are edible and others are poisonous! Remember to never eat a berry unless an adult who knows plants very well tells you it's OK to eat. Salmonberry is a berry that is edible and looks and tastes like a pinkish-orange raspberry. Many berry plants look similar, but salmonberry is the only one that has a "butterfly" hiding in its leaves (can you see the leaf butterfly in the photo?).

BIG-LEAF MAPLE

Can you figure out why this maple is called big-leaf maple? Not only does this tree have the best and biggest leaves around our area, but it also has helicopter seeds that are fun to drop off bridges and decks! They swirl and spin in a mesmerizing way through the air in the fall. Big-leaf maples are really tall when they're full-grown, but one trick to tell them apart from other giant forest trees is to look at the trunk. Big-leaf maples almost always have more moss on their trunks than any of the other trees.

Nature Boat

If you've ever visited a stream, river, or creek, you've probably sent leaves and sticks floating down it. Can you combine a few different natural objects to create a boat that floats? It may be harder than it seems—your boat might take on water and sink, or it may tip over! Keep trying and see if you can learn from a boat that doesn't float (think about why it may have sunk or tipped). For an extra challenge, try to make a boat without the use of hot glue—use only natural objects to bind together. If you don't have access to outdoor water, such as a pond, lake, creek, river, or stream, you can always test your boats in the bathtub.

MATERIALS

☐ Natural objects   ☐ Hot glue gun (optional)

☐ Stream, river, creek, lake, or bathtub

DIRECTIONS

1. Gather objects from the ground outside that you might want to use to make the boat. Examples include pinecones, leaves, bark, sticks, and flowers.

2. Decide how you'd like to put together the boat, either with glue or without glue. If you want to use hot glue, ask an adult to glue the pieces together with a hot glue gun.

3. Allow the boat to dry for several hours. If you used hot glue, wait until an adult says that the boat is cool enough to handle and then test it in water.

4. Please remember that we do not want to leave glue in outdoor water sources, so if you send a boat down a stream, river, or creek, have someone standing a bit further down ready to catch it. If you create a boat entirely with natural materials, it is safe to leave it.

Extensions

RACE TWO DIFFERENT BOATS. WHICH ONE IS FASTER? WHY DO YOU THINK SO?

CREATE THE TALLEST BOAT YOU CAN THAT DOES NOT TIP OVER.

CREATE THE LONGEST BOAT YOU CAN THAT DOES NOT LEAK.

Dandelion Bubbles

Dandelions are weeds, but they are also pretty neat plants. For instance, every part of a dandelion is edible! Because these plants are safe to put in your mouth, and because they have hollow stems, they make amazing bubble blowers. When you make your dandelion bubble blower, be sure to save the flowering head of the dandelion for the bonus activity below!

MATERIALS

☐ Dandelion(s)   ☐ Dish soap   ☐ Water   ☐ Dish

DIRECTIONS

1. Pick a tall dandelion at the bottom of the stem or uproot the whole plant.
2. Cut off the flower at the top of the stem and make a second cut at the bottom of the stem.
3. Rinse the dandelion stem in the sink.
4. Mix a small amount of dish soap with a small amount of water.
5. Dip one end of the dandelion stem in the dish soap mixture and swirl it around so it is completely coated.

6. Lift the stem out and blow slowly through the non-soapy end of the stem. A bubble should begin to form!

7. Experiment with different mixtures of dish soap and water, different lengths of dandelion stems, and different speeds of blowing air through the stem. Which combinations make the biggest bubbles? Which make the longest-lasting bubbles?

Extensions

CAN YOU FIND OTHER NATURAL OBJECTS TO MAKE INTO BUBBLE BLOWERS? (REMEMBER TO ASK AN ADULT TO CHECK AND MAKE SURE THAT A PLANT ISN'T POISONOUS OR HARMFUL BEFORE PUTTING IT IN YOUR MOUTH.)

BONUS ACTIVITY

Place the flowering top of the dandelion in a cup with water so that the stem is in the water and the flower is out of the water. Keep it in a sunny place and watch what happens as the flower goes to seed.

Plaster Treasures

Plaster is an interesting medium to work with because it sticks to any kind of nature treasure you can find without the use of glue. You can use the plaster like a blank canvas and arrange your treasures in a pattern or picture, or you can use the plaster to keep all your treasures in one place. This is a great way to display a collection of objects from a vacation or special trip.

MATERIALS

☐ Plaster of paris   ☐ Water   ☐ Plastic container   ☐ Natural objects

DIRECTIONS

1. Collect a wide range of natural objects. Keep in mind that objects like rocks stay the same over time, whereas delicate treasures like flowers eventually wilt.

2. Grab a plastic container from your recycling bin. Make sure it has no holes or cracks and be sure to wash and dry it.

3. In a bowl, mix 2 parts of plaster of paris for every 1 part of water. Stir well until there are no lumps and the plaster of paris powder is evenly distributed.

4. Pour the plaster of paris mix into the plastic container.

5. Work quickly to place your treasures. Plaster starts to set after 5 to 10 minutes. If you'd like more time to work, add slightly more water to the plaster mix and mix well.

6. Allow your work to dry for several hours or overnight.

7. If you'd like to retrieve your objects, tip the container over and gently tap to loosen the objects.

Extensions

CAN YOU MAKE SYMMETRICAL ART WITH NATURAL OBJECTS AND THE PLASTER?

WHAT HAPPENS IF YOU PLACE A LEAF ON THE SURFACE OF THE PLASTER, ALLOW THE LEAF TO DRY OUT, AND THEN PICK AT THE DRY LEAF TO REMOVE IT?

CAN YOU BUILD A TALL CREATION USING THE PLASTER AS THE BASE?

Story of the Lake

This is an interactive story where you'll get to see what happens over time to a once-wild lake as people begin living nearby without thinking of the lake. Start with a bowl of water (clean lake) and read this story aloud. When you are prompted, add the various materials to the bowl of lake water. This activity is a great introduction to local water quality testing (page 60).

MATERIALS

☐ Bowl filled with water   ☐ "Pesticides" and "fertilizers" (food coloring or paint)

☐ Small cup of "sawdust" (bread crumbs, potato flakes, actual sawdust, flour, etc.)

☐ Small cup of "dirt" (actual dirt, cinnamon, cocoa powder, etc.)

- [ ] "Soaps" (soap or shampoo)   - [ ] "Oils" (cooking oil or baby oil)
- [ ] "Poop" (raisins, chocolate sprinkles, etc.)

Once upon a time, there was a lake. No one lived by the lake. It was filled with clear, clean water (1. admire your bowl of clean water). The animals on the land near the lake drank and played there and ate the many fish that thrived in the lake. Surrounding the lake were great forests of tall, green healthy trees and these trees were homes to many forest creatures.

One day, people moved near the lake. They drank water from the lake and lived in the forests and decided that this lake was a wonderful place to live near. More and more people came and after some time, the people needed to build many houses. They built a sawmill near the lake and cut down giant patches of the forest. The sawmill dumped lots of sawdust into the lake (2. add the "sawdust"), which made it harder for the fish of the lake to see and breathe. Fall came and rain fell on the big blank patches of land where the trees used to be. There were no longer trees to hold the dirt in place with their strong roots, and lots of dirt ran down the hills into the lake (3. add the "dirt"). This made it even harder for the fish and other lake creatures to see and breathe.

The people living around the lake made large farms to grow food. They used pesticides to keep bugs out of the food and fertilizers to make their food grow bigger and faster. As the rain fell, it washed some of the pesticides and fertilizers off the plants and into the lake (4. add the "pesticides" and "fertilizers"). The pesticides began to poison fish and lake creatures, causing some of them to die. The fertilizer made a type of plant called algae grow out of control on the surface of the lake. The algae used up a lot of the oxygen in the water, making it even harder for the few fish and creatures in the lake to breathe and survive.

The number of houses and roads began to grow and the number of cars grew as well. The city installed storm drains to keep the roads and sidewalks from flooding when it rained. When it rained, oils that the cars had left behind on the roads traveled through the storm drains to the lake (5. add the "oils"). People washed their cars with soap in their driveways and that soap ran down the roads, to the storm drains, and ended up in the lake (6. add the "soap"). This further hurt the fish and other lake creatures. The forest wildlife no longer drank or played at the lake as often because the water was not as fresh and clean.

The people who lived in the cities around the lake had a sewer system that emptied into the lake and they had pet dogs they didn't pick up after. All of this poop made its way into the lake (7. add the "poop"). The lake was no longer safe to play in—people who ventured in became quite ill.

The people began to realize that their lake was sick. They started to find ways to help the lake by changing what they did. They stopped cutting trees in big groups all at once and instead cut a few trees at a time. They planted new trees to grow in the empty spaces of land. They gathered the sawdust from their mills and dumped it in the garbage instead of in the lake. They added native plants and planted a wetland around the lake. The wetland plants began to clean some of the pollution out of the lake (8. scoop out some of the pollution from the bottom of the lake).

The people created new drains that brought their sewage to a treatment plant to clean the water. They labeled their storm drains so everyone could read about where the water from their neighborhood streets and sidewalks was going. They started to pick up after their dogs. They washed their cars at car washes where the soapy water drained to a treatment plant instead of into the lake. The farms that grew food for the people began to use fewer pesticides and chemicals.

Over time, with the help of plants, bacteria, and less incoming pollution from the people, the lake began to get healthier. The people added fish and the water was clean enough that the fish could live there. Other lake creatures returned, and the animals began to visit the lake again.

The people learned how to take care of the lake and they taught their children how to care for it too, so the lake, animals, forest, and people could live happily ever after!

BONUS ACTIVITIES

Find out where your storm drains lead. Does the water from your neighborhood affect a stream, lake, river, or ocean?

Go for a walk around your neighborhood. Are the storm drains labeled? If they are not, most cities have a program that provides volunteers with a method of labeling if you are willing to do the work.

Does your city provide a Pet Waste Station with free bags to dispose of pet waste? Visit a local trail or park and see if you can find one. If not, consider working with your city to add them.

Decorated Sticks

Wrapping and decorating sticks with embroidery thread or yarn or string is a peaceful activity that creates gorgeous art to display in your home!

MATERIALS

☐ Fallen sticks

☐ Glue

☐ Colored yarn or embroidery thread or string

☐ Scissors

DIRECTIONS

1. Collect fallen sticks.
2. Choose a material to wrap around a stick. (Thick yarn is easiest for younger children, whereas older children may enjoy the challenge of thinner embroidery thread.)
3. Tie a double knot where you'd like to start wrapping and place a dot of glue on the knot.
4. Cut off any excess thread or yarn.
5. Wrap the thread or yarn over as much of the stick as you'd like, tie another double knot, and add another dot of glue on the knot.
6. Cut off any excess thread or yarn.
7. Repeat as many times as you'd like.

BONUS ACTIVITY

Paint and decorate fallen sticks, bark, or other natural objects such as leaves or acorn tops.

Earthworm Tower

Earthworms are an important part of the underground world. Not only do they break down dead materials like fallen leaves and change them into soil, they also add air to the soil by making tunnels. In the earthworm tower, you can watch the fallen leaves seemingly disappear over time as the earthworms eat them and turn them into soil. You can also see the tunnels that the earthworms make that add air to the soil, making it healthier for plants!

MATERIALS

- [ ] Clear 2-liter plastic bottle
- [ ] Dried leaves
- [ ] Sealed ½-liter plastic bottle
- [ ] Soil
- [ ] Sand
- [ ] Scissors
- [ ] Earthworms

DIRECTIONS

1. Rinse and dry a clear 2-liter plastic bottle and a sealed ½-liter plastic bottle. Remove any labels on the 2-liter bottle.

2. Ask an adult to use a drill or nail to make several air/drainage holes along the bottom of the 2-liter bottle.

3. Ask an adult to cut off the top quarter of the 2-liter bottle with scissors.

4. Place the sealed ½-liter bottle inside the 2-liter bottle so that it is nested in the center of the larger bottle.

5. Add alternating layers of sand and soil into the space between the small bottle and the large bottle until the top of the smaller bottle is covered.

6. Add enough water to moisten the soil and sand.

7. Add a final layer of crumbled dried leaves once you get near the top of the large bottle.

8. Add anywhere between one and five earthworms to the top of the leaves.

9. Cover the bottle loosely with dark paper if you'd like to see tunnels near the surface of the bottle. You can slide the paper off when you want to peek at the earthworms. If you do not cover the bottle, the earthworms may tunnel near the center of the bottle because they shy away from sunlight.

10. Periodically check on the tower. Can you see earthworms? Can you see the tunnels they've left behind? How does the size of the pile of dried leaves change over time?

Texture Garden

Nature offers such a variety of textures—rough, smooth, fuzzy, ridged, and even bumpy! In this activity, you'll create a miniature garden to explore with your hands. If you live in a wet environment, you may wish to collect mosses as we've done. If you live in a dry environment, you may wish to collect sedum. If you don't have easy access to either, you can order them online or find them at a gardening store.

MATERIALS

☐ Recycled container or reused container from a thrift store ☐ Soil

☐ Sedum or mosses ☐ Spray bottle ☐ Rocks

DIRECTIONS

1. Find and clean a container from your recycling bin or go on a thrift store hunt. A shallow container will work as long as it has edges to hold in soil and water.

2. Add a layer of rocks for drainage at the bottom of the container.

3. Add a layer of soil to cover the rocks.

4. Add patches of different textures of moss or sedum to fill in the container.

5. If you planted a moss garden, spray daily with water just until moist. If you planted a sedum garden, water every few days.

6. You can keep the planter indoors or outdoors as long as it has access to sunlight.

BONUS ACTIVITIES

Go on a texture scavenger hunt and find as many different textures as you can.

Take a small sample of various natural textures from your yard and make a texture board or texture cards by gluing them down to cardboard or index cards. You could even make sets of matching index cards and create a texture matching game.

Water Cycle Demonstrations

All the water on Earth moves through the water cycle. A drop of water may spend time as part of a cloud and then rain before it soaks into the ground as groundwater, only to be sucked up by a tree root and "sweat" out of the tree on a hot day, returning to the cloud to rain down on a lake. The following two demonstrations help you see how water can move from liquid to vapor (gas), and back to liquid again.

WATER CYCLE IN A BAG

In this demonstration of the water cycle, you will create a miniature Earth! The water at the bottom of the mountain represents groundwater. Groundwater is literally water that you find underground. Communities that drink water from wells are drinking groundwater. The remaining water at the bottom of the bag represents a lake. As the sun (or heat from a hair dryer) heats up the groundwater and lake water, some of the water turns to vapor. Water can also turn to vapor from trees as they sweat out water from their leaves. The water vapor travels to the top of the bag where the "clouds" are and then it cools and turns to "rain." Over time you can see rain traveling down from the clouds to the mountain and trees.

MATERIALS

- [ ] Ziplock bag
- [ ] Permanent marker
- [ ] Water
- [ ] Tape
- [ ] Blue food coloring (optional)
- [ ] Hair dryer (optional)

DIRECTIONS

1. Draw a mountain on one side of the bag—the mountain should be less than half the size of the bag. Draw trees. Draw a sun in an upper corner of the bag. Draw a few clouds at the top of the bag near the sun.

2. Add 5 tablespoons of water to the bag. Add 2 drops of blue food coloring (optional).

3. Seal the bag to trap additional air inside (so the sides of the bag don't stick together).

4. Tape the bag to a window so the sun is at the top of the bag and the water is at the bottom.

5. Allow the sun to heat the water over time. To speed up the heating process, use a hair dryer (optional).

WATER CYCLE IN A CUP

In this demonstration the cup represents a simple miniature Earth. Rather than focusing on how the sun heats the water, this demonstration focuses on how the clouds cool the water vapor. The water in the bottom of the cup represents a lake. The ice on top of the plastic wrap represents the cold temperatures up in the atmosphere where clouds are.

MATERIALS

- [ ] Cup
- [ ] Plastic wrap
- [ ] Rubber band
- [ ] Ice
- [ ] Blue food coloring (optional)

DIRECTIONS

1. Pour approximately ½ cup of water into a small cup. Add 2 drops of blue food coloring (optional). This water represents the lake.

2. Cover the top of the cup with plastic wrap. Hold it in place with a rubber band.

3. Add 1 or 2 pieces of ice on top of the plastic wrap. This represents cold temperatures in the clouds where water vapor travels. These cold temperatures cause the water vapor to condense and become rain.

4. Check on the water cycle cup after 15 to 20 minutes. Can you see rain forming at the bottom of the plastic wrap cloud?

Nature Sensory Bottles

Sensory bottles are a good way to focus on the details of natural objects, such as the wrinkly textures on a lichen-covered twig or the detailed vein patterns on a leaf. They are also a wonderful way to safely introduce babies and young toddlers to objects from nature that should not go in their mouths. In addition to providing a way to study nature at its prime, sensory bottles are an interesting way to study how natural items decompose over time.

MATERIALS

☐ Empty plastic bottles (we used VOSS BPA-free plastic bottles)

☐ Distilled water   ☐ Natural objects

DIRECTIONS

1. Go on a hunt for interesting natural objects. Be sure that whatever you choose can be folded or otherwise squeezed through the opening in the plastic bottle.

2. Rinse the natural objects.

3. Fill the plastic bottle with distilled water (distilled water stays clear the longest).

4. If the opening of the bottle is small, ask an adult to carefully fold and add the natural object.

5. Seal the bottle. If a baby or small child is in the house, ask an adult to add a bead of super glue between the lid and bottle to keep it sealed. Young children should always be supervised with these bottles.

Extensions

WHAT KINDS OF NATURAL OBJECTS BREAK DOWN THE FASTEST?
WHICH ONES BREAK DOWN THE SLOWEST?

COMPARE AN UNRINSED OBJECT IN ONE BOTTLE TO A RINSED VERSION
OF THAT OBJECT IN ANOTHER BOTTLE. WHICH ONE BREAKS DOWN FASTER?

MAKE A SET OF BOTTLES EACH SEASON TO HIGHLIGHT HOW NATURAL
MATERIALS CHANGE THROUGHOUT THE YEAR.

Nature Blocks

What blocks are better to keep outdoors than blocks made from trees! These blocks are a great way to give old, dead branches a new life, and to learn a little more about the insides of trees in the process. Get creative with many different block shapes and sizes. If possible, use branches from two or more different types of trees for comparison. Also try to cut at least one thin disc-shaped cross-section of a branch to study.

MATERIALS

☐ Old tree branches

☐ Sandpaper or sander

☐ Clamp and hand saw or table saw

DIRECTIONS

1. Collect large dead tree branches that are dry.
2. If you have a table saw, ask an adult wearing protective eyewear to cut blocks of different sizes and shapes from the branches. If you do not have a table saw, use a clamp to hold a branch in place and ask an adult wearing protective eyewear to use a handsaw to cut blocks of different sizes and shapes.
3. Ask an adult to use sandpaper or a sander to smooth any rough edges that may give you splinters.

LEARNING ABOUT TREE RINGS

Using a disc-shaped piece from the branch, take a closer look. Trees add a ring of growth for every year. How old is the branch you're looking at? Count the rings to find out. Rings also tell us about the type of year the tree had. If a certain ring is especially thick, there was a lot of rain and sun that year and the tree was able to grow much bigger. If a ring is thin, there was a drought or other hardship that kept the tree from growing much that year.

Surfaces Demonstration

Before there were people and cities, there was wide open space with a lot of plant growth. When cities were built, roads, sidewalks, and other manufactured surfaces were laid over the dirt, natural grasses, and native plants. When rain falls on impermeable surfaces such as roads and sidewalks, it runs off the road instead of soaking into the dirt and being used by the plants and grasses. This creates a problem—we don't want all that water flooding our roads and houses! So we created storm drains. These drains collect the water that runs from our sidewalks and roads and move it to a natural space, such as a river, lake, or even the ocean. In this demonstration, you'll see why sidewalks and roads can be problematic when pollution is introduced (from car exhaust, oils, garbage, pet waste, and more).

MATERIALS

- [ ] Patch of grass and dirt
- [ ] Sidewalk or road
- [ ] "Pollution" (ideas: cornstarch, liquid watercolors, water)

DIRECTIONS

1. Find a patch of grass and a sidewalk or road—you will run the demonstration in these two locations.

2. Mix up the pollution. We made ours by mixing ¼ cup of cornstarch with ½ teaspoon of washable liquid watercolors and ⅓ cup of water. Whatever you choose, be sure to make two containers with equal amounts of the same pollution in each.

3. Slowly pour the pollution on the sidewalk or road. What happens? Where does the pollution go? What do you think will happen when it rains?

4. Slowly pour the pollution over the patch of grass. What happens here? How is it different? What do you think will happen when it rains? Why do you think having grass and dirt (natural land) around might be important to handling pollution?

5. Check back over time to see how the pollution looks in each location after various amounts of time (days/weeks) have passed.

Extensions

NOT ALL NATURAL SURFACES ARE EQUAL—SOME ABSORB MORE WATER. CAN YOU FIND A NATURAL SPACE THAT ABSORBS EVEN MORE WATER THAN THE GRASS PATCH? BASED ON WHAT YOU FIND, CAN YOU GUESS WHAT THE IDEAL SURFACE WOULD BE TO SOAK UP RAINWATER?

BONUS ACTIVITIES

Take a walk around your neighborhood with your eyes on the sides of the road. Where is the closest storm drain?

Find out where the water from your neighborhood roads and sidewalks ends up. If the storm drain is labeled, you can easily see where it empties. If it's unlabeled, you can either call the city for more information, or look at a map of your area—whatever the closest large waterway is to your home is likely the exit point of any water that enters the storm drain.

Go for a drive through a more populated part of your town and look at the sides of the roads. Do you see any ditches with wetland plants (such as cattails)? If so, your city is trying to help the problem of roads. The water from all the roads surrounding the ditch empty into it. Cattails and other wetland plants are pretty special—they can help absorb and break down some of the pollution coming from the roads. With their help, cleaner water enters a drain and heads to the nearest waterway.

Nature Cutting Tray

Scissor skills are important to practice with children, and combining scissor practice with nature gives kids a new way to explore natural materials. Cutting leaves (especially those of herbs) can often release wonderful smells; cutting apart flowers or other plant structures can give children a way to study the various parts of a plant.

MATERIALS

☐ Tray   ☐ Kid-safe scissors   ☐ Plant clippings

SAFETY NOTE

Please make sure the plants you gather for the cutting tray are not poisonous or otherwise dangerous for children.

DIRECTIONS

1. Go on a hunt for plant parts in your yard. Keep in mind that kid-safe scissors do best with thin plant parts and aren't able to cut through woody structures.

2. Place the cuttings on a tray with kid-safe scissors.

3. Explore!

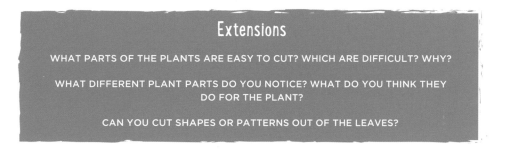

Extensions

WHAT PARTS OF THE PLANTS ARE EASY TO CUT? WHICH ARE DIFFICULT? WHY?

WHAT DIFFERENT PLANT PARTS DO YOU NOTICE? WHAT DO YOU THINK THEY DO FOR THE PLANT?

CAN YOU CUT SHAPES OR PATTERNS OUT OF THE LEAVES?

BONUS ACTIVITY

Use the more fragrant cuttings to make smelling bottles. Older children may enjoy closing their eyes and trying to identify scents from the smelling bottles. You could even make a scent-matching game.

Frog Hunt

How sharp are your eyes? Can you find all the hidden frogs? In this activity, an adult hides plastic frogs outside. You'll pretend to be a frog predator (something that eats frogs) and collect prey (something that is eaten—in this case, frogs!) in a jar. As you go hunting, notice which kinds of frogs are easy to find and which are harder.

MATERIALS

☐ Plastic frog set   ☐ Jar or container   ☐ Backyard or other open natural space

DIRECTIONS

1. Ask an adult to hide the frogs outside in a certain place. Make sure they count how many they've hidden so you know how many there are to find.

2. Head out with the jar and hunt for frogs! Which frogs did you find first? Where did you find them and what did they look like? Which frogs were hardest to find? Where did you find them and what did they look like?

BONUS ACTIVITIES

The frogs that were hardest to find were probably camouflaged. This means they were colored the same or similar to their surroundings (grass, leaves, or dirt) and blended in. Many prey animals use camouflage to hide from predators. Go on a nature walk and look closely at the trees and plants and grasses—can you find a real-life prey animal that is camouflaged? (Hint: many insects rely on camouflage to stay safe from predators).

Were the frogs that were easiest to see brightly colored? If yes, they are probably models of real-life brightly colored frogs called poison dart frogs. They don't rely on camouflage as much, but instead they rely on their bright colors to warn predators that they are poisonous! Poisonous prey animals tend to be brightly colored. Predators have learned over time that bright colors means they should stay away. Go on a hike and see if you can find examples of brightly colored creatures. Do a little research to see if their bright colors are meant to advertise that they are poisonous.

Nature Weaving

Weaving is a beautiful way to create art. In this activity you'll get to create and decorate a natural loom using plants and other objects from nature. As you weave objects into the loom, pay attention to which objects are easiest to weave and which are most difficult. Over time, what happens to the objects you've woven? Do they wilt? What types of natural objects last the longest in the nature loom?

MATERIALS

☐ Sticks ☐ Yarn ☐ Hot glue

☐ Objects for weaving (ideas: feathers, sticks, vines, flowers, leaves, etc.)

DIRECTIONS

1. Lay the sticks out to create a square or rectangular shape (or whatever shape you'd like to create), and make sure the sticks slightly overlap.

2. Have an adult add hot glue where the sticks overlap and allow the hot glue to dry.

3. Further reinforce the corners by wrapping them with yarn.

4. Tie a knot with the yarn at the top corner of the shape and, keeping tension in the yarn, slowly wrap it around the whole frame, leaving space between each yarn wrap.

5. Once you've wrapped the whole frame, tie a final knot in the yarn and you're ready to weave!

6. Go on a hunt for natural objects that might work for weaving.

7. Though a weave is intended to be used in an over, under, over, under alternating pattern, feel free to explore different ways of adding natural materials to the loom.

8. Don't forget that the loom is reusable—when you're ready to try new weaving, just remove the old objects.

Extensions

CAN YOU BRAID, WEAVE, OR KNOT NATURAL OBJECTS TOGETHER WITHOUT USING A LOOM? TRY CREATING ART OR NECKLACES BY MAKING A DAISY OR CLOVER CHAIN, OR ANOTHER COMBINATION OF NATURAL OBJECTS.

Investigate a Snail

Snails and slugs are often thought of as garden pests (which they are), but in nature they have important jobs. Their waste and their bodies (after they die) are a source of nutrition for plants, and they are a tasty snack for animals. They also work hard as decomposers—living creatures that work to break down rotting material, such as old leaves and branches. Snails and slugs move using one large "foot," a muscle that runs along the bottom of their bodies. They also use slime, which helps them move along any surface you can think of. Their slime trails also communicate to other snails or slugs: "good food this way!" or "danger—predator ahead!" Though they can't see colors, they have two eyes on stalks that can sense light and retract into their heads if they get poked.

MATERIALS

- [ ] Snail or slug
- [ ] Magnifying glass (optional)
- [ ] Sheet of clear plastic (from your recycling bin or a sheet of plexiglass from the local hardware store)

DIRECTIONS

1. Coax or pick up and place the snail/slug on a sheet of plastic. Watch how it moves by looking at the underside of the plastic. Can you see its foot muscle working to move it forward?

2. Investigate different angles. Can the snail/slug climb straight up? What about upside down?

3. Investigate its sense of light and dark. What happens if you quickly move your hand by its head?

4. If you'd like to hold the snail/slug, hold it gently and allow it to move on your hand. Can you feel its foot muscle working? When you're done, you may find that its slime is hard to remove from your hand. A scrub brush or textured sponge work best at removing slime. Always be sure to wash your hands after handling snails/slugs.

Extensions

JUST LIKE PLANTS, CREATURES LIKE SNAILS AND SLUGS CAN BE NATIVE OR INVASIVE. SEE IF YOU CAN FIGURE OUT WHETHER THE SNAIL OR SLUG YOU STUDIED WAS NATIVE OR INVASIVE. IF IT WAS INVASIVE, GO ON A HUNT TO SEE IF YOU CAN FIND A NATIVE SNAIL OR SLUG!

FIND ANOTHER CREATURE IN YOUR YARD AND STUDY IT. WHAT DO YOU NOTICE ABOUT THE CREATURE?

Wild Seeds

Plants rely on seeds to spread out so they can sprout and grow new plants in new places. Some seeds rely on wind to carry them to far-off places, whereas other seeds rely on rivers or streams to float downstream before finding a place to sprout. Others rely on animals to transport them, either by sticking to their fur or traveling in their stomachs after being eaten and waiting to be pooped out! For this activity you'll go on a seed hunt and choose one or more seeds to sprout and grow.

MATERIALS

☐ Newspaper   ☐ Large bottle or glass   ☐ Soil   ☐ Miscellaneous seeds

DIRECTIONS

1. To make a pot for the seeds, first lay out a sheet of newspaper horizontally.

2. Lay a large glass or bottle on one end of the newspaper so the bottom of the glass/bottle is about halfway down the sheet of newspaper.

3. Hold one end of the newspaper against the bottle and begin to roll it. It should create a hollow tube of newspaper around the bottle.

4. Once you've completely rolled up the newspaper, fold in the bottom half against the bottle so that you create a solid bottom to the newspaper pot. Once you fold in the bottom portion of the newspaper, put the bottle upright and press down firmly to further compact the bottom of the newspaper pot.

5. Slide out the bottle and add dirt to the newspaper pot.

6. Go on a nature hunt for various types of wild seeds.

7. Make guesses as to how the seeds find new homes to sprout in. Are any of the seeds part of a fruit? If so, they are planning to travel in animal's stomachs. If the seeds float, they are likely to rely on wind or water to move to new places.

8. Plant your seeds by burying them under about ½ inch of soil in your newspaper pot. Place the pot somewhere sunny and warm and keep the soil moist by watering as needed. In a few days or weeks, you should see a new baby plant sprout up!

Sticky Nature Bracelet

A sticky bracelet is a fun way to collect treasures that you find on a walk or hike. As the seasons change, so does your sticky bracelet! Take photos of the bracelet as the months go on and see how the selection of natural objects varies depending on the month.

MATERIALS

☐ Colored cardstock paper ☐ Contact paper ☐ Scissors

DIRECTIONS

1. Cut a strip of cardstock long enough to fit around your wrist.
2. Cut a strip of contact paper that is approximately 1 inch wider than the strip of contact paper.

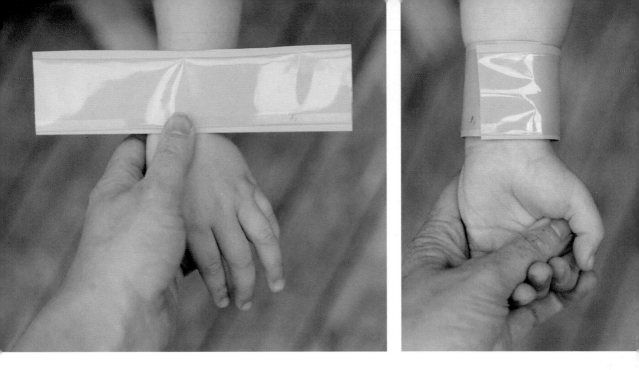

3. Peel the backing off the contact paper and face it sticky side out.

4. Fold the upper ½ inch of the contact paper over and use it to stick the contact paper (sticky side out) to the upper edge of the cardstock.

5. Fold the remaining bottom strip of the contact paper over and press so that the contact paper sits against the cardstock.

6. Wrap the bracelet, sticky side out, around your wrist. Use scissors to cut off any excess bracelet.

7. Collect natural objects to decorate the bracelet.

8. Notice which objects stick and which don't. If you have an object that is large (such as a large flower), it is unlikely to stick unless you use a smaller piece of it (such as a petal).

Extensions

ASK AN ADULT TO CAREFULLY CUT THE STICKY BRACELET OFF YOUR WRIST.
ADD A TOP LAYER OF CLEAR CONTACT PAPER, STICKY SIDE DOWN, TO HOLD YOUR
NATURAL TREASURES IN PLACE. USE SCISSORS TO TRIM THE EDGES DOWN TO THE SIZE
OF A BOOKMARK. AS AN OPTIONAL STEP, USE A HOLE PUNCH AT THE TOP CENTER
AND TIE A STRING OR RIBBON IF YOU'D LIKE TO ADD A PORTION TO THE BOOKMARK
THAT STICKS OUT.

Rainbow Photo Challenge

There are so many vibrant colors in nature. Whether you're looking at rocks, shells, flowers, plants, or even little creatures—you can always find a rainbow! For this challenge you'll collect photos rather than objects. This is a great opportunity for older children to learn to use a camera and take photos themselves. Or an adult can be their historian. A fun way to end the project is to create a photo collage with your findings.

MATERIALS: Camera

DIRECTIONS

1. Over time (weeks, or even months!) take notice of the colors in the world around you. Don't limit yourself to just plants—check out feathers, living creatures, and objects like rocks and shells. When you find something with a color of the rainbow (red, orange, yellow, green, blue, or purple), take a picture of it.

2. Once you've gathered many photos, use a photo-editing software to create a photo collage. If you're not sure how to make a photo collage, see Appendix A for resources.

Extensions

ADD THE COLORS BROWN, GRAY, BLACK, AND WHITE TO YOUR HUNT.

COLLECT PHOTOS FOR A YEAR OR UNTIL YOU GET A CERTAIN NUMBER OF PHOTOS OF OBJECTS OF EACH COLOR (FOR EXAMPLE, KEEP HUNTING UNTIL YOU FIND 20 RED OBJECTS, 20 ORANGE OBJECTS, ETC.)

GO ON A RAINBOW LEAF HUNT IN THE FALL.

BONUS ACTIVITIES

Go on a pattern hunt and try to find natural objects that are striped or polka-dotted or otherwise patterned.

Go on a shape hunt and find objects that are a certain shape. Heart-shaped hunts are one of our favorites.

Sweating Leaves Demonstration

Did you know that trees sweat? It's true! Trees are an important part of the water cycle. The water that evaporates (or turns to invisible water vapor) from their leaves can travel up to become part of a cloud, which could become rain, which could then fall and be soaked up by plant roots and start the journey all over again (see page 32 for two demonstrations of the water cycle). In fact, it's estimated that 15% of the water vapor in the sky comes from the leaves of trees and other plants! It's hard to imagine water evaporating from tree leaves—so let's prove that it happens by catching the water vapor in the act.

MATERIALS

- ☐ Clear plastic bag
- ☐ Rubber band or twist tie
- ☐ Leaves that are still attached to a tree

DIRECTIONS

1. Find a tree in your yard or nearby and choose a spot on the tree where you can reach a handful of leaves.

2. Take the clear plastic bag and, leaving the leaves on the tree, bundle a few up inside the plastic bag.

3. Gently fasten the plastic bag so that it won't slip. This doesn't need to be absolutely airtight to work, but it needs to be tight enough that the bag won't fall off if there's any wind or rain overnight.

4. Notice what the leaves and bag look like now—even better, take a picture of what they look like—and then leave them overnight.

5. The next day, come back and check the bag. You should see a fair amount of water in the bottom of the bag. How did it get there? The tree leaves sweat it out! The bag prevented the water vapor from evaporating into the air and instead caused the water vapor to condense and become water again (like how rain forms in clouds).

6. Remove the bag from the leaves.

Extensions

COMPARE A FEW DIFFERENT TYPES OF TREES. TRY TO GATHER THE SAME AMOUNT OF LEAVES IN EACH BAG AND LEAVE THEM FOR THE SAME AMOUNT OF TIME. DO SOME TREES SWEAT OUT MORE WATER? WHAT KIND OF LEAVES DO THEY HAVE? WHAT KIND OF LEAVES DON'T SWEAT OUT AS MUCH WATER?

BONUS ACTIVITY

Is the water that evaporates from the ocean salty? Find a large empty container and make sure to rinse and clean it. Mix about 2 cups of warm water with about ¼ cup of salt. Stir well to dissolve the salt and add the warm salty water to the container—this represents the ocean. Place a glass (or another small, heavy container that fits inside the large container) in the center of the large container filled with warm water. Cover the top of the large container with plastic wrap and seal the edges with tape or secure the plastic wrap with a rubber band. Place a weight (like a small rock) on top of the plastic wrap toward the center. The weight should cause the plastic wrap to dip down toward the small, heavy glass container that sits in the center of the large container. Leave it for several days. Once a good amount of rainwater has fallen from the plastic wrap clouds into the glass container, remove the glass container, and take a sip. Is the water freshwater or saltwater?

Seed Bomb Lollipops

Seed bomb lollipops make great creative gifts. You can fill them with any sort of seed you'd like, from native wildflower seeds to garden plants (such as lettuce, carrots, nasturtiums, etc.) and more. Once they've been made (and dried out), all you have to do is plant them upside down in soil. You can either remove the lollipop stick or use it as the base for a plant label. If you plant the seed bomb lollipop outside, plant it in the late spring or summer for best results. You can sprout and grow the seed bomb lollipops indoors year-round if you have a sunny window for the sprouts.

MATERIALS

☐ Two pieces of 8.5 x 11-inch recycled paper or colored paper ☐ Water ☐ Bowl

☐ Biodegradable lollipop sticks (not the plastic kind) ☐ Seeds of your choice

DIRECTIONS

1. Tear the first sheet paper you'd like to use into small pieces with your hands (or you can cut it up with scissors) and add all the pieces to a bowl.

2. Tear the second sheet of paper in half and then tear each half into long strips. The size of the strips can vary a bit—they don't need to be exact. Set these strips aside.

3. Add 3 tablespoons of water to a bowl and mix it into the small paper pieces with your hands. After a minute or two, this should start to feel mushy, like paper pulp.

4. Gather half of the paper mush in one hand and squeeze it gently to remove a bit of the water. Place 5 to 8 seeds in the center of the paper mush.

5. Place the remaining paper mush on top so the seeds are sandwiched between the two handfuls of paper mush.

6. Squeeze the paper mush firmly into the shape of a ball in your hands. You should be squeezing hard enough to remove more water.

7. Use one hand to brace the ball of paper mush while you push a lollipop stick into the center of the ball. Squeeze again to secure the ball onto the lollipop stick.

8. Gently set the ball of mush on the lollipop stick aside and add the strips of paper to the water left in the bowl (add more water if needed) and flip them from side to side until they are wet and soaked with water.

9. Pick up the ball of paper mush in one hand and place the wet strips of paper one at a time over the outside of the paper ball. They can overlap, but aim to cover as much of the paper ball as you can with the wet paper strips.

10. Once you have placed the paper strips on the ball, squeeze it once more to remove any extra water.

11. Set the wet seed bomb lollipop on a paper towel and let it dry for 24 to 48 hours.

Underwater Viewer

An underwater viewer is a quick project that allows you to easily cut the glare from the sun to get a better look at what's going on in any kind of water—a pond, puddle, stream, or lake!

MATERIALS

☐ Scissors   ☐ Plastic wrap   ☐ Rubber bands

☐ Plastic or otherwise waterproof container from your recycling bin (old milk cartons or large plastic jars or bottles work well)

DIRECTIONS

1. Search through your recycling bin for a waterproof container that is large and tall.

2. Rinse it well and ask an adult to cut open the top and bottom of the container with scissors so that it forms a viewing tunnel.

3. Tear off a piece of plastic wrap that is approximately twice as large as one end of the open container.

4. Center the plastic wrap piece over one end of the opening in the plastic container.

5. Place a rubber band over the plastic wrap to hold it in place against the container. If the rubber band isn't thick or tight, you may want to use more than one to keep the plastic wrap in place.

6. Pull the ends of the plastic wrap until the portion that is covering the opening is taut with no wrinkles.

7. Place the plastic wrap viewing window down in the water you want to investigate. Place your head in the opening and push down until the viewer is slightly under the surface of the water. Investigate!

Extensions

CAN YOU THINK OF ANOTHER CLEAR SURFACE OTHER THAN PLASTIC WRAP THAT YOU COULD USE TO MAKE A VIEWING WINDOW? TRY THAT AND COMPARE IT TO THE PLASTIC WRAP VIEWING WINDOW. WHICH VIEWER WORKS BEST?

CAN YOU THINK OF ANOTHER WAY TO MAKE AN UNDERWATER VIEWER? TRY TO MAKE IT AND COMPARE TO THE ORIGINAL. WHICH WORKS BEST?

MAKE SKETCHES OF WHAT YOU SEE IN YOUR NATURE JOURNAL.

Stream Water Quality

If you live near a stream, creek, or river, water from your neighborhood drains from the roads and sidewalks to the storm drains, and from there it likely drains to the stream. This local stream is in your care (and the care of your neighbors)! You can check and see how healthy a nearby stream, creek, or river is with simple tools. Scientists have more advanced and more accurate ways to test water quality, but even without those testing methods, we can make a great guess as to how healthy your local stream or creek is by doing the activities below. The more activities you complete, the more information you'll have. More information helps you make a better guess about how the stream is doing.

SAFETY

Unfortunately, many of the world's streams are not healthy. As a precaution against potential infection, I recommend wearing gloves while interacting with the water, particularly if you have any open cuts or wounds. As an added precaution, always wash your hands and anything else that has been exposed to the water.

STREAM CHECKLIST

Take a look at the picture of the stream on the previous page. This photo includes many hints that tell us the stream is healthy. When you visit the stream, count how many hints it has from the checklist below. The more you find, the healthier the stream is:

- ☐ Shade: Healthy streams have shade from nearby trees and plants. Shade keeps the water temperature from getting too high on sunny days. The higher the water temperature, the less air (oxygen) there is for the creatures that live in the stream to breathe.

- ☐ Plants and logs: Healthy streams have fallen logs, branches, and nearby plants. These break down into nutrients for stream bugs and plants to use to grow. The plants and logs also serve as hiding places for fish and other stream creatures.

- ☐ Riffles: Riffles are little ripples in the stream. They add air (oxygen) to the water for the creatures living there to breathe through their gills.

- ☐ Shape and speed of the stream: Twisty and bendy (meandering) streams are healthier than straight streams. Walk along the stream and see if you can find different water speeds. There should be little pockets of almost-still water along the sides and faster-moving water toward the center. Different stream creatures need different speeds of water to do well. If the stream has a lot of different water speeds, it's likely home to many different kinds of stream creatures.

- ☐ Bottom of the stream: Do you see many different objects at the bottom of the stream, such as plants, large rocks, small rocks, dirt, and even wood (branches or logs)? If so, there is likely to be a wider variety of stream creatures living there. If your stream is home to fish, having gravel or rocks (instead of just sand) along the bottom is vital to the health of their eggs. Too much sand makes it too hard for fish eggs to breathe and they will die.

MEASURING TURBIDITY

Turbidity is a fancy word for the cloudiness of water. Very cloudy water (high turbidity) makes it hard for stream bugs, fish, and other creatures to breathe. To breathe, they filter water through their gills, and these bits and pieces in the water can clog their gills. Cloudy water also makes it hard for sunlight to get through the water to any underwater plants that are trying to grow in the stream. Fewer plants in the water means less food for many of the creatures that live in the stream. Finally, the more cloudy the water, the warmer it tends to be. The warmer the water, the less oxygen it holds. This means that anything trying to breathe with gills gets less air when the water is cloudy and warm.

Scientists use tests to determine the percentage of turbidity. For our test, we'll use a modified version of a Secchi disk—a black-and-white disk used to test how well you can see through water.

MATERIALS

- [ ] Tall clear plastic cup or jar with a flat bottom
- [ ] White paper
- [ ] Permanent black marker
- [ ] Scissors
- [ ] Stream water
- [ ] Tape
- [ ] Sink water

DIRECTIONS

1. Set the bottom of the cup on a piece of white paper and use a marker to trace around the outside bottom.

2. Cut out the circle of paper you've traced.

3. Draw a plus sign with the marker so the center of the plus sign is roughly in the center of the paper circle and the lines of the plus sign extend to the edges of the circle.

4. Color two opposite quadrants of the circle in with black marker.

5. Tape the circle (colored side up) inside the cup on the bottom so that when you look in the cup, you see the pattern of alternating black-and-white quadrants.

6. Fill the cup to the top with clear water from a sink. Notice how easy it is to see the black-and-white pattern on the bottom of the cup.

7. Fill the cup to the top with water from a stream. How hard is it to see the black-and-

white pattern? The easier it is, the less cloudy (turbid) the water is and the healthier the stream is. Please note that colored water is not the same as cloudy water. In the fall, many streams collect a high number of fallen leaves and those leaves release tannins, which can give a brownish color to the water. This is not harmful to living creatures. What is harmful is sand, silt, or other floating particles—these are what make it hard for living things in the stream to breathe.

MEASURING TEMPERATURE

If you've checked the turbidity of the stream, you probably already have a guess as to whether the stream temperature is high or low (hint: the cloudier the water is, the warmer it is). Warmer water is harder on living creatures in the stream because it holds less air (oxygen) for them to breathe through their lungs.

MATERIALS: Thermometer

DIRECTIONS

1. Place the bulb (the bottom part) of the thermometer completely underwater. You may wish to use a rock or two to hold the thermometer in place.

2. Leave the thermometer for about 5 minutes to give it a chance to measure the temperature of the water.

3. Read the thermometer. Healthy cold-water streams should be 68 degrees Fahrenheit or lower. Healthy warm-water streams should be 89 degrees Fahrenheit or lower.

MEASURING PH

Another way to measure the health of a stream is to measure the pH level. However, pH is pretty complicated, so for our purposes we'll just learn that living things need a neutral pH to survive. A low pH number (acidic) or a high pH number (basic) means that it's unlikely that creatures can live in the stream.

MATERIALS

- [ ] pH paper strips
- [ ] Cup
- [ ] pH key (this comes with pH paper strips)

DIRECTIONS

1. Fill a cup about half full with the stream's water and dip a pH paper strip in it.

2. Remove the paper pH strip and place it on the side of the cup.

3. Hold up the key and match the color of the pH strip with a color on the key.

4. What color and number on the key match the stream? A pH level below 5 likely means that the stream is too acidic for living creatures to survive; a pH level over 9 likely means that the stream is too basic for living creatures to survive. If the pH number is between 5 and 9, the stream is likely to be neutral enough for living creatures. The ideal pH level is 7. The closer the pH level is to 7, the healthier it is.

MEASURING MACROINVERTEBRATES

Macroinvertebrates is the fancy name for little stream bugs that live underwater. These little guys breathe through gills and are, in many cases, the baby versions of bugs that fly around streams—mayflies, dragonflies, caddis flies, and more! Not only are stream bugs fun to hunt and hold, they are a great way to check the health of your stream. Stream bugs also are a vital food source for any fish that may live in the streams. The more pollution-intolerant and varied stream bugs in a stream, the more likely there are fish in there somewhere too!

MATERIALS

- [ ] Water-friendly shoes
- [ ] Underwater viewer (optional; directions on page 58)
- [ ] Macroinvertebrate identification chart (Appendix B)
- [ ] Cup (optional)
- [ ] Small and clean soft-bristled paintbrush

DIRECTIONS

1. Though you can find macroinvertebrates in any part of a stream, one of the easiest places to find them is along the edge of a stream. Find large rocks and gently remove them, turning them over as you do. If you can get to a riffle—a shallow area where there are small ripples— you will find more macroinvertebrates.

2. Keep a close eye on the bottom sides of the rocks. If you see any movement, it's likely to be a macroinvertebrate.

3. Some macroinvertebrates are large enough that you can identify them while they cling to the wet rock. If the stream bug you've found is small or if you'd like to take a closer look, use the soft-bristled end of a small paintbrush to gently brush the stream bug off the rock and into the palm of your hand or a cup filled with stream water. If you use your hand to hold the bug, make sure that you have a bit of stream water to cover it. Stream bugs are very delicate, so please handle them as gently as possible so you don't harm them.

4. Watch the stream bug closely. You should be able to see it breathe through its gills, small feather-like structures on the side of its body. The bug uses its gills to filter air (oxygen) out of the water. This is how it breathes to stay alive.

5. Compare the stream bug to the pictures of different bugs on the macroinvertebrate identification chart at the back of the book (Appendix B). Which does it look like? What group of insects does it belong to? If you find a stream bug in group 3, this doesn't necessarily mean that the stream is polluted—these creatures can be found in all kinds of streams—even healthy ones. However, if you find a macroinvertebrate in group 1, it likely means that the stream is fairly free of pollution, as the little stream bugs in group 1 can only tolerate a small amount of pollution before they die off.

Nature Crown

Decorate yourself with nature by making beautiful nature crowns. This easy craft takes just a few minutes. It's a great addition to a photoshoot or creative imaginative play. Nature crowns can be used time and again and are a fantastic way to display the beautiful natural finds of every season.

MATERIALS

☐ Sticks   ☐ Hot glue gun   ☐ Natural objects   ☐ Scrap paper

DIRECTIONS

1. Take a piece of scrap paper and cut it into two strips. Tape one end of one strip to the end of another strip to create a long piece of paper.

2. Ask an adult to use the long piece of paper to measure around your head where you'd like the crown to rest. Add a piece of tape so the circle of paper holds its shape and remove it from your head.

3. Break up 5 to 7 sticks and lay them, overlapping slightly, so that they form a circle the same size as the paper circle you created in step 2.

4. Ask an adult to add a generous amount of hot glue wherever the sticks overlap.

5. Take another stick and break it into two pieces approximately 4 inches long.

6. Ask an adult to set the two pieces as an upside down V at the front of the crown and glue them wherever the sticks cross.

7. Allow the crown to cool.

8. Collect natural objects you'd like to use for the crown. Decide where to place them and then ask an adult to add a dot of hot glue to affix them to the crown.

9. Allow the crown to cool completely before placing it on your head.

Extensions

CAN YOU CREATE A CROWN USING JUST KNOTS, TWISTS, OR BRAIDS—BUT NO GLUE— TO HOLD THE CROWN TOGETHER?

WHAT TYPES OF NATURAL OBJECTS LAST THE LONGEST ON THE CROWN? WHICH WILT OR TURN BROWN MOST QUICKLY? WHY DO YOU THINK THIS HAPPENS?

Sink and Float

Sometimes heavy objects float (like boats) and light objects sink (like a small coin). This is because whether an object sinks or floats doesn't have to do with how heavy it is, but rather how dense it is. Density is the measure of how much stuff there is in a given space. The more stuff there is in a space, the more dense it is. When an object is more dense than water, it sinks. In this activity you will find natural objects that sink and float.

MATERIALS

☐ Natural objects   ☐ Water   ☐ Bowl or container

DIRECTIONS

1. Fill a bowl or container with water.
2. Go on a hunt for natural objects.
3. Add the objects you've collected to the container of water and watch whether they sink or float.

Extensions

TRY PLANT SEEDS. WHY DO YOU THINK IT'S HELPFUL FOR SEEDS TO FLOAT RATHER THAN SINK?

CAN YOU USE OTHER NATURAL OBJECTS TO MAKE SOMETHING THAT NATURALLY FLOATS SINK? CAN YOU USE OTHER NATURAL OBJECTS TO MAKE SOMETHING THAT NATURALLY SINKS FLOAT?

Rain Drums

Rainy days may seem less exciting for outdoor play, but there are plenty of fun activities to do in the rain. One of our favorite ways to play in the rain is to bring out the rain drums. Different storms make different songs, so letting the rain play our drums is always an adventure.

MATERIALS

☐ Plastic containers

☐ Balloons of various sizes

☐ Scissors

DIRECTIONS

1. Wash and dry the plastic containers.

2. Gather balloons that are the correct sizes for the openings of the containers.

3. Using scissors, cut the bottom off the balloon as shown in the photo.

4. Use your hands to stretch the balloon so that it completely covers the opening of the container. The balloon will grip the sides once you let go.

5. Take the rain drums outside and place them balloon side up in the rain. The harder the rainfall, the louder your drums play.

6. What do you notice about how sound changes as the shape of the drum changes?

7. Experiment with coverings other than balloons. Do they work? Why do you think this is?

BONUS ACTIVITIES

What other instruments can you make using natural objects?

Have the rain contribute to your artwork. Draw a picture with washable markers on watercolor paper and place it on a tray in the rain for a few minutes. What happens? Another way to try rain painting is to place a piece of watercolor paper on a tray and add food coloring, liquid watercolors, tempera paint powder, or small bits of watercolor paint cakes to the paper and leave it in the rain for a few minutes. Try a few different methods to see which results you like best!

If it snows or hails, gather some in a container and paint it with watercolors, tempera paint, liquid watercolors, or diluted food coloring.

Pounding Art

Plant flowers are beautiful to look at. Using a hammer, paper towel, and watercolor paper, you can make a permanent print of the bright colors of flower petals. Test a variety of flowers and see if you can find out which types of petals transfer the best. Many different flowers work well, but to get you started, we'll share two of our favorite flowers for pounding—violas and cosmos. These flowers aren't found in the wild, but they are popular at garden stores and farmers' markets. They can also be easily grown from seed in a pot or garden if you'd like to have your own crop of flowers for pounding.

MATERIALS

- ☐ Flowers
- ☐ Hammer or mallet or meat pounder
- ☐ Watercolor paper
- ☐ Paper towels or napkins

DIRECTIONS

1. Decide whether you'd like to transfer a whole flower or a petal (you can experiment with both to see which you like better). Place either the flower or the petal facedown on your watercolor paper.
2. Fold up napkins or paper towels and place them over the flower/petal.
3. Being careful of fingers, pound all over the paper towel until the entire flower or petal is pounded. (Young children should have adults pound for them)
4. Remove the paper towel or napkin.
5. Carefully peel what remains of the flower or petal away to reveal the pounded flower print.

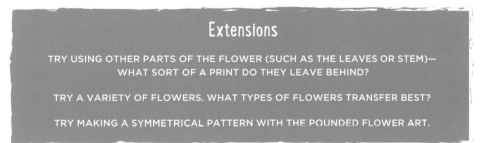

Extensions

TRY USING OTHER PARTS OF THE FLOWER (SUCH AS THE LEAVES OR STEM)—
WHAT SORT OF A PRINT DO THEY LEAVE BEHIND?

TRY A VARIETY OF FLOWERS. WHAT TYPES OF FLOWERS TRANSFER BEST?

TRY MAKING A SYMMETRICAL PATTERN WITH THE POUNDED FLOWER ART.

Coloring Flowers

Have you dyed white flowers by adding food coloring to the water they are in? In this activity we'll see whether the amount of food coloring we add to the water changes how thoroughly the flower petals are dyed.

MATERIALS

- ☐ Three cut white flowers
- ☐ Food coloring
- ☐ Scissors
- ☐ Water
- ☐ Plastic water tubes (optional but handy—we buy ours from a florist)

DIRECTIONS

1. Gather three cut white flowers. Chrysanthemums, morning glories, carnations, and daisies all work well for this experiment. If you don't have any of these flowers in your yard, one or more types are typically available in grocery stores year-round.

2. Decide which color of food coloring you'd like to use to dye the flowers.

3. Decide how many drops of food coloring you'd like to use in each cup. We tried 1, 5, and 10 drops of food coloring.

4. Add the same amount of water to each of the 3 cups (or water tubes).

5. Add the drops of food coloring to each cup. Label the cups as you go. (We labeled ours 1 drop, 5 drops, and 10 drops).

6. Use scissors to cut the stems so they are approximately 5 inches long.

7. Place one flower in each cup.

8. Let them sit overnight and check back in the morning.

9. Compare the three flowers—which flower has the most dye in its petals?

10. Because a flower, even one that has been cut, needs water to keep from wilting, the flower moved water from the cup up through the stem to its petals. When the flower moved the water up, it took some of the dye with it. That dye stayed in the flower petals.

Extensions

CAN YOU DYE FLOWERS THAT AREN'T WHITE? TRY USING THE METHOD ABOVE TO SEE WHAT HAPPENS.

CAN YOU DYE OTHER PLANT PARTS (LIKE LEAVES?). TRY USING THE METHOD ABOVE TO SEE WHAT HAPPENS.

Rolling Nature Painting

Though this activity is fun for all ages, it's perfect for some of the youngest artists who love to shake! Experiment with different kinds of natural objects to see how the prints vary. Does your print change if the objects are spiky versus smooth? What about large versus small objects?

MATERIALS

☐ Round natural objects   ☐ Watered down washable paint   ☐ Lid   ☐ Tape
☐ Disposable foil baking tray with clear plastic lid   ☐ Paper   ☐ Scissors

DIRECTIONS

1. Go on a hunt for natural objects that easily roll. You may choose rocks, seedpods, empty snail shells, pinecones, or anything else!

2. Take a disposable foil baking tray and cut a piece of paper so that it fits snugly on the foil bottom.

3. Tape the paper to the bottom of the foil tray.

4. Mix a small amount of water into the paint—just enough to make the paint drip slowly off a mixing spoon (some brands of washable paint won't need water, but if the paint is thick enough to cling to a spoon it probably needs water).

5. Add small pools of paint on the white paper.

6. Add whatever rolling natural objects you'd like to the bottom of the tray.

7. Click the lid onto the tray and shake, roll, and move the tray however you'd like.

8. Open the lid, remove the natural objects, and carefully remove the paper artwork from the bottom of the tray.

9. Rinse the tray to reuse later. You can either keep the natural objects painted, or if you'd like to return them outdoors, rinse them as well.

Extensions

TRY LINING A COFFEE CAN OR OTHER CANISTER FROM YOUR RECYCLING BIN WITH PAPER, PLACING PAINT AT THE BOTTOM, ADDING NATURAL OBJECTS, THEN CLOSING THE LID AND SHAKING IT. HOW DOES YOUR ART COMPARE TO THE ART PRODUCED BY THE METHOD ABOVE?

ADD PAPER TO A RAMP OR SLIDE, DIP NATURAL OBJECTS IN PAINT, AND ROLL THEM DOWN THE RAMP OR SLIDE TO CREATE ART.

Acrylic Paint Sun Prints

This technique is one of the most beautiful ways to make natural art that I've ever seen! In this activity we use it to make T-shirts, but you could use it to make prints on anything cotton—dish towels, pillows, and more!

MATERIALS

- [ ] Cotton T-shirt
- [ ] Paintbrush
- [ ] Plastic bag or tarp
- [ ] Flat natural objects
- [ ] Acrylic paint
- [ ] Spray bottle
- [ ] Water
- [ ] A sunny day

DIRECTIONS

1. Go on a hunt for flat natural objects. Leaves work well. Try to select objects that lay flat against the T-shirt for the best results. For example, a rose would not work well for making a print, but a single rose petal would.

2. Thoroughly wet the T-shirt under a faucet. Gently squeeze the excess water out. The shirt should be wet, but not dripping.

3. Lay the shirt out facing up on a plastic bag or tarp.

4. Mix the acrylic paints so they are very watery. A good rule of thumb is to add about as much water as there is paint. You do not need to be exact with this measurement. Be sure to stir well so that there are no lumps in the paint. Please note that yellow or light pastel colors do not show the prints as well as darker colors do.

5. Paint the entire front of the shirt.

6. Using a spray bottle filled with water, spray 2 to 3 coats of water over the surface of the wet painted shirt.

7. Place the natural objects facedown (or whatever the flattest side is down) and press gently. Press all the edges completely into the wet painted T-shirt. If it is a windy day, use small rocks or other weights to keep the leaves and other objects in place.

8. Leave the T-shirt in a sunny place for several hours (or all day!).

9. Once the T-shirt is dry to the touch, carefully peel the natural objects from the shirt to reveal the beautiful prints left behind.

10. The natural objects kept the areas of the shirt they covered wet for longer than the rest of the shirt. The uncovered areas of the shirt began to dry more quickly, and as they did, they drew the water, and much of the paint, out from under the natural materials. Thus the paint moved from under the leaves and other objects out to the rest of the shirt and dried there, leaving a less painted space under the objects.

Find something that smells sweet	Find something that feels rough	Find something that's spiky
Find something that's smooth	Find something you can climb on	Find something you can balance on
Find something brightly colored	Find something making noise	Find something that flies
Find the tallest living thing you can	Find the smallest living thing you can	Find something that crawls
Find something that feels warm	Find something that feels cold	Find something you can hide under

Outdoor Scavenger Hunt

Scavenger hunts are a fun way to draw your attention to the details of an outdoor space. They also work as great motivation to keep younger kids engaged in a hike or long walk. This outdoor scavenger hunt is open-ended and can be used many times in different environments. If you'd like to bring a copy of it with you, you can photocopy the opposite page (and even laminate it for long-term use) and pack it!

MATERIALS: Copy of the scavenger hunt on the opposite page.

Extensions

MAKE THIS A PHOTO SCAVENGER HUNT BY TAKING A PICTURE OF EACH OBJECT YOU FIND.

BONUS ACTIVITY

Go on an indoor scavenger hunt for the following objects in your house (you may not have all of them):

☐ Toothpaste   ☐ Sunscreen   ☐ Shampoo   ☐ Salad dressing
☐ Yogurt   ☐ Vitamins   ☐ Ice cream ☐ Peanut butter

These all (usually) contain ingredients that come from the ocean! The next time you're in a car at night, notice how the street signs reflect light from the car's headlights—that's thanks to the shells of tiny ocean creatures called diatoms! A mixture of their shells coats street signs and that coating makes the street signs easier to read when driving at night!

Make a Bug Hotel

Bugs are such an important part of any outdoor environment. They pollinate flowers, provide food for other outdoor creatures, and break down dead leaves and sticks. We need bugs for our outdoors to stay healthy! In this activity, you'll get to create a bug hotel in your backyard. You can try lots of different objects and check back to see if any bug friends have moved in! By providing shelter (and sometimes a food source), you're helping to keep the bugs, and therefore your outdoor environment, healthy!

MATERIALS

☐ Container for the bug hotel (ideas: cardboard box, self-made wood box using wood scraps, wood container from thrift store, or terra cotta pots)

☐ Natural materials to put inside a bug hotel (ideas: sticks, cut branches with or without drilled holes, pinecones, chemical-free sawdust, grass, dead leaves, hay, moss, lichen, bamboo pieces, cardboard pieces, recycled paper or newspaper shreds, etc.)

DIRECTIONS

1. Decide what container to use for the bug hotel. Does it have compartments already? If not, find a way to make compartments (cardboard or wood dividers work well).

2. Choose a natural material for each compartment. If you'd like to drill holes in any pieces of wood, be sure to ask an adult to drill the holes.

3. Stuff each compartment full of a natural material.

4. Place the bug hotel in a natural place in your backyard (ideally in the dirt for maximal exposure to bugs).

5. Check back periodically. How will you decide which material the bugs like best? Will you observe over time, or will you unpack the materials after a certain number of days?

6. Were you able to tell if certain bugs liked certain materials? Is this similar to where you find them in nature?

Extensions

GO ON A BUG HUNT IN YOUR YARD OR AT A LOCAL PARK. HOW MANY DIFFERENT KINDS OF BUGS CAN YOU FIND? WHERE DO YOU FIND THE MOST BUGS?

Recycled Paper Postcards

Old printer paper, old art projects, old newspapers, and various scraps left over from art projects can all be recycled into handmade paper postcards. After making and decorating the postcard, use it to send a note to a parent, grandparent, or one of your friends!

MATERIALS

- [ ] Two craft felt sheets
- [ ] Window screen (or wire mesh)
- [ ] Towel or cotton rag
- [ ] Recycled paper
- [ ] Blender or bowl
- [ ] Water
- [ ] Pressed flowers (optional) or plant seeds (optional)

DIRECTIONS

1. Gather old paper and tear it into small pieces using your hands or cut it into small pieces using scissors.
2. Add approximately ½ cup of water for every 1 cup of shredded paper.
3. Either use a blender to blend the water and paper until it's smooth or, after allowing the paper to soak for 30 minutes, use your hands to break up the paper until it's smooth.
4. Cut a piece of window screen or mesh and lay it on top of a towel or cotton rag.
5. Scoop or pour the smooth paper pulp onto the window screen or mesh.

6. Use your hands to spread the pulp so that it is evenly distributed across the window screen or mesh. Aim for a ½-inch or 1-inch thick pile of pulp.

7. Lay one of the felt craft sheets over the evened out layer of pulp and press down.

8. As you compact the pulp by hand, the excess water should squeeze out through the window screen or mesh into the towel. The fine mesh should retain the paper pulp.

9. Once the paper pulp is nice and flat and you've squeezed out as much water as you can, gently lift it using the corners of the mesh and lay the paper pulp, pulp side up, on top of the second (dry) piece of felt. Leave the window screen or mesh attached to the bottom of the paper pulp.

10. If you wish to add seeds to the postcard to make it plantable, press seeds into the damp pulp now.

11. Smooth any wrinkles or tears by pressing down with your fingers and leave the paper to dry for 24 hours.

12. After 24 hours check to be sure the paper is dry. If it is dry to the touch, flip the paper over (so the paper is facedown) and gently peel back the window screen or mesh.

13. Use scissors to cut the postcard to size. The US Postal Service accepts postcards that are 4 inches wide by 6 inches long.

14. If you'd like to add pressed flowers or leaves, place them on the postcard and then paint a layer of glue over the entire surface of the postcard to hold them in place.

15. Write a note on the postcard, add a stamp, and mail it to surprise someone you care about!

Nature Potions

Making nature potions and perfumes was one of my favorite activities as a child. In this activity you will have a chance to tear, smoosh, mix, and mash natural materials to create exciting concoctions!

MATERIALS

☐ Bowl or cup or other container   ☐ Water   ☐ Natural materials

DIRECTIONS

1. Fill the container with water
2. Add whatever natural materials you'd like!

Extensions

CAN YOU MAKE A POTION THAT NATURALLY COLORS
THE CLEAR WATER YOU STARTED WITH?

CAN YOU MAKE A POTION THAT SMELLS DELICIOUS USING JUST NATURE?

CAN YOU MAKE A POTION THAT YOU THINK WOULD HELP A PLANT GROW?

CAN YOU MAKE A POTION THAT YOU THINK BUTTERFLIES WOULD LIKE?

CAN YOU MAKE A POTION THAT IS YOUR FAVORITE COLOR?

Leaf People

Can you make pretend people using leaves and other natural materials? Could you make yourself out of leaves? What about your whole family? This is a great activity to celebrate the colors of fall and to study the shapes and sizes of leaves in any season!

MATERIALS

- [ ] Clear contact paper (this can be found online, at craft stores, or sometimes in the kitchen shelf covering aisle of a large store)
- [ ] Leaves and other natural materials
- [ ] Googly eyes (optional)

DIRECTIONS

1. Go on a hunt to gather leaves of different sizes, shapes, and colors. Keep an eye out for other interesting natural materials that could be useful for decorating leaf people.

2. Design a leaf person by laying out the leaves and other pieces on the ground the way you'd like them.

3. Cut a piece of clear contact paper that's bigger than the leaf person and remove the paper backing. Lay the contact paper on the ground, sticky side up.

4. Transfer the leaf person piece by piece from the ground to the sticky paper.

5. Once everything is in its place, cut a second piece of contact paper that's the same size as the first. Peel the paper backing off and lay it sticky side down over the top of the leaf person.

6. Press the two pieces of contact paper together firmly.

7. Trim around the leaf person, taking care to leave a 1- to 3-inch border around the edges of the leaf person.

8. Add googly eyes if you wish.

BONUS ACTIVITIES

Use glue to glue leaves of different shapes, sizes, and colors to a sheet of white paper. Draw with a marker to create a person, creature, or other picture that includes the leaves.

Gather natural materials and try to create 3-D creatures out of them. Ask an adult to help you keep the pieces in place with a hot glue gun. You can add googly eyes at the end if you wish.

Mystery Games

Everyone loves a good mystery, right? Can you identify something just by touch? Can you remember what went missing? In these activities you'll need to rely on your memory and senses to solve the puzzle.

FIND A TREE

This activity is ideal in an open space with different kinds of trees. Parks are perfect because they are usually thoughtfully landscaped with a variety of trees.

MATERIALS

- ☐ Trees
- ☐ Blindfold
- ☐ Partner

DIRECTIONS

1. Look around and choose a tree.
2. Go up to the tree and touch it, smell it, and listen. Try to memorize the sounds around the tree, the smell of the tree, and the texture of the tree.
3. Take 20 steps away from the tree.
4. Have your partner blindfold you and spin you around (gently) several times.
5. With your partner guiding you (and keeping you safe from branches or holes or other things that might cause you to fall), try to find your way back to the tree.
6. Once you think you've found the tree, remove your blindfold and see if you were correct.
7. Switch roles with your partner and play again!

WHAT'S MISSING?

This game is a test of memory—can you tell which of the natural objects has gone missing?

MATERIALS

☐ Natural objects (young children will likely be challenged by 3 or 4 different objects, whereas older children and adults may need 6 to 12 objects to be challenged)

☐ Partner ☐ Place to sit

DIRECTIONS

1. Gather natural objects and bring them to a place where you can comfortably sit.
2. Sit facing your partner with about 2 feet of space between you.
3. Have your partner arrange the natural objects in the space between the two of you.
4. Take a minute or two to memorize what is there. When you're ready, turn your back to your partner (no peeking!).
5. Your partner should remove one of the objects, hide it somewhere out of sight (such as behind their back), and let you know it's time to turn back around.
6. Turn back around and try to guess what is missing!
7. For more of a challenge, use more objects or have your partner scramble the remaining objects before you turn back around, or both.
8. Once your turn is over, switch roles with your partner so they have a turn!

Can you identify one object just by touch? What about several objects? Put yourself to the test in this game of blind guessing.

MATERIALS

☐ Bag or pillowcase (that you can't see through)   ☐ Natural objects   ☐ A partner

DIRECTIONS

1. Gather natural objects with your partner and place them all inside the bag or pillowcase.
2. Have your partner hold the pillowcase and, without peeking, reach your hand in and grab something.
3. With your hand still inside the bag and without looking, guess which object you've grabbed.
4. Remove the object to see if you were right!
5. Put it back in the bag and shuffle the objects before giving your partner a turn.
6. For an added challenge, collect a bag of objects out of view of your partner and ask your partner to do the same. Try to guess the objects, without knowing what went into the bag!

Nature Wreath

Gather beautiful natural objects that celebrate the season and place them on a cardboard wreath frame to bring beauty to your front door! This is yet another way to celebrate the seasonal changes of the outdoor world.

MATERIALS

- [ ] Cardboard (at least 12-by-12 inches)
- [ ] Pushpin
- [ ] String
- [ ] Marker
- [ ] Hot glue
- [ ] Scissors or box cutter
- [ ] Natural objects

DIRECTIONS

1. Cut a length of string that's about 12 inches long.
2. Tie a knot around a pushpin at one end of the string.
3. About 9 inches down the string (from the pushpin), tie a knot around a marker.
4. Using one finger to press the pushpin down in the center of the cardboard, pull the string taut and draw a circle on the cardboard using the marker.
5. Slip the marker out of the knot and tie it onto the string near the end.
6. With the pushpin still in the center of the cardboard, pull the string taut and draw a second larger circle around the first circle using the marker.
7. Ask an adult to use a box cutter or sharp scissors to cut out the cardboard wreath.
8. Gather all the natural objects and ask an adult to glue them with a hot glue gun to whichever spots you choose on the cardboard wreath.
9. For the fullest-looking wreath, try to cover all the cardboard with natural objects.

Make a Terrarium

One of the most important groups of creatures on our planet are the decomposers. They work with bacteria, fungus, and mold to break down old plant and animal material. When they break down these materials, they clean up what would otherwise make a giant (and smelly!) mess and they return important nutrients (like vitamins) to the soil to grow healthier plants.

SAFETY: Many decomposers are friendly, but some can bite (such as ants and centipedes).

MATERIALS

- [ ] Container that allows air circulation
- [ ] Dirt
- [ ] Dead leaves
- [ ] Rotting wood
- [ ] Moss
- [ ] Isopod or other decomposers

DIRECTIONS

1. Create a home for the decomposers by adding dirt, dead leaves, rotting wood, and moss.

2. Add decomposers. Isopods (which are known by many names including wood lice, roly-polies, pill bugs, and potato bugs) make a great choice as they do not bite and are not poisonous.

3. Observe the decomposers—what do they do, what do they eat, where do they sleep?

4. If you have isopods (roly polies), gently turn them over and check underneath them near their back legs. If you see two white dots, those are eggs. If you see tiny white bugs crawling around the bottom of your isopod—those are baby isopods!

5. If you'd like to keep them for more than a day or two, please be sure to add enough water that the terrarium is damp but not wet and make sure they have at least two food sources (rotting wood and dead leaves are good examples).

Extensions

GO ON A HUNT FOR DECOMPOSERS. LOOK IN DIFFERENT PLACES (FOR EXAMPLE, UNDER A BIG ROCK, UNDER A LOG, IN A PILE OF DIRT, UNDER A PILE OF LEAVES, ETC.) AND COUNT HOW MANY ISOPODS YOU FIND IN EACH LOCATION. CAN YOU TELL WHAT THEIR FAVORITE PLACE TO LIVE MIGHT LOOK LIKE BASED ON THE NUMBERS YOU COUNTED?

Bird Beak Game

There are so many different birds in the world of various colors, shapes, and sizes. In this activity we'll look at why birds have beaks of different sizes and shapes. You get to act like a hungry bird and experiment with different types of beaks to hunt for food. See if you can figure out why the shape of a bird's beak and the food it eats are related!

MATERIALS

- [ ] Pretend food (ideas: cereal, noodles, pipe cleaners, pom poms, raisins, goldfish, paper fish, small toy fish, small toy insects, water, marbles, paper clips, etc.)
- [ ] Pillowcase or sheet (optional)
- [ ] Stopwatch (optional)
- [ ] Pretend beaks (ideas: straws, spoons, forks, tweezers, pipettes, clothespins, etc.)
- [ ] Cup or bowl for each person playing

DIRECTIONS

1. Decide which materials to use for the pretend bird food and which beaks to test.

2. Gather pretend bird food and lay it on the ground (or on a sheet on the ground).

3. Choose a pretend bird beak to use and try to gather as much food as you can in 30 seconds. Move the food you catch with your beak to the cup.

4. After the 30 seconds is up, talk about which food type was easiest to get with your beak. Why?

5. Repeat steps 3 and 4 for each beak type.

6. What did you learn? Were certain foods easier with certain beaks?

7. Take a look at pelicans online or in a book. What kind of beak do they have? What do they eat? How does this help them? Look up sandpipers and hummingbirds and answer the same questions.

Extensions

VISIT THE LOCAL PET STORE AND CHECK OUT THE BIRDS. DO ALL THE BIRDS HAVE THE SAME KIND OF BEAK, DESPITE BEING DIFFERENT SIZES AND SHAPES AND TYPES OF BIRDS? WHAT DO THEY ALL EAT? WHY DO YOU THINK THEY ALL HAVE SIMILAR BEAKS?

BONUS ACTIVITY

An owl is a type of bird that eats smaller animals whole. It cannot digest the bones or fur of the creatures it eats, so as a result, it produces an owl pellet. Owl pellets can be dissected to find the bones of the creatures the owl has eaten. Use a bone chart to guess how many creatures the owl has eaten and what kinds of creatures they were (mice and voles are the most common meals). You can purchase sterilized owl pellets online or at a science supply store.

Create Bird Feeders

What style of feeder will attract the most birds? Do certain kinds of birds like certain feeders? Do some birds eat from any kind of feeder? Find the answers by creating bird feeders using craft supplies, natural materials, and objects from your recycling bin!

MATERIALS

- [ ] Clean and dry containers from your recycling bin
- [ ] Twine or yarn or string
- [ ] Pipe cleaners
- [ ] Sticks
- [ ] Recycled paper towel tubes
- [ ] Fruit rinds
- [ ] Pinecones
- [ ] Mixed birdseed from a local store
- [ ] Anything else you can think of

DIRECTIONS

1. Use the gathered materials to make bird feeders of different shapes and sizes.
2. Fill the bird feeders with seeds.
3. Place them in a tree, hang them from a roof or window, or place them on a deck. Be sure to keep them close together so the birds can choose the one they want.

4. If you haven't fed birds before, it make take several days before they notice the feeders and realize there are seeds there, so you may need to be patient.

5. Observe the birds from a distance or periodically check the amount of seeds left.

6. What feeders were most popular? Was there one in particular that many birds visited or that ran out of seeds first?

7. Were you able to see any birds eating? What did you notice about the size or type of bird and which types of feeders they preferred?

Extensions

TRY SEVERAL DIFFERENT BIRD FOODS AND SEE IF THERE'S A CERTAIN TYPE OF SEED OR FOOD THAT THE BIRDS LIKE BEST. IDEAS FOR FOODS TO TRY INCLUDE UNSALTED PEANUT BUTTER, UNSALTED PEANUTS, MIXED BIRD SEED, THISTLE SEED, SUNFLOWER SEEDS, WATER-SOAKED RAISINS, FRESH APPLES OR ORANGES, PEANUT BUTTER MIXED WITH CORNMEAL (ONE PART PEANUT BUTTER TO EVERY FIVE PARTS CORNMEAL), UNSALTED PUMPKIN SEEDS, ETC. IF YOU'D LIKE TO TRY A DIFFERENT FOOD OTHER THAN THE ONES LISTED, PLEASE CHECK TO BE SURE THAT IT IS SAFE AND HEALTHY FOR BIRDS TO EAT.

Nesting Materials
for Birds

In the spring, the neighborhood birds scavenge the outdoors in search of the perfect nesting materials. Each type of bird (species) builds its nests a little differently. Some birds use mud, some use mud and sticks, some use yarn and fur and feathers, and so on! In this activity you'll figure out what nesting materials the neighborhood birds like most. And if you're really lucky, you might spot a nest with your materials!

MATERIALS

- [ ] Paper towel or wrapping paper or toilet paper cardboard tubes
- [ ] Natural materials (ideas: chemical-free pet fur, non-dyed feathers, strips of cotton fabric, cotton batting, straw, dry grasses, sticks, short strips of cotton yarn, short strips of string, wool felt, moss, etc.)
- [ ] String
- [ ] Scissors

DIRECTIONS

1. Think about what natural materials birds might want to use for their nests. Avoid anything that doesn't break down (such as nylon or polyester fibers) and avoid anything brightly colored (so the nests don't attract the eyes of predators). Also keep any strings or yarn short in length (a few inches only) so the birds don't become entangled in them.

2. Cut the cardboard tubes at approximately 1-inch intervals.

3. Squeeze one 1-inch thick cardboard circle so that it fits through another 1-inch thick cardboard circle at a right angle.

4. Stuff the sphere made by the two cardboard circles with one of the materials you've selected. Repeat to create several spheres, each with one material inside.

5. Tie a length of string through the top of the filled sphere and tie the opposite end from a tree branch or roof or another structure where birds can see it.

6. Check back periodically after several days. Have some materials been taken more often than others? Are any of the spheres empty? Can you catch any of the neighborhood birds in the act of taking materials for their nests?

BONUS ACTIVITY

Research what kinds of native birds are in your area. With the help of an adult, research what kind of nesting box one of the local species of birds needs (see Appendix A). The size and shape and location of a birdhouse varies depending on the type of bird! Once you've gathered this information, work with an adult to build a nesting box specifically for a local bird species!

Foil Leaves

Foil leaf imprints are a great way to preserve the beauty of leaves. In the leaf imprint, you'll notice all the intricate veins that moved water and food throughout the plant. This activity is a great way to use your sense of touch to explore the many details of leaves.

MATERIALS

☐ Piece of cardboard   ☐ Aluminum foil   ☐ Permanent markers

☐ Leaves   ☐ Glue

DIRECTIONS

1. Gather a few different types of leaves for the imprints. Choose one leaf to start with.

2. Cut a piece of cardboard about the same size as the leaf.

3. Place a dot or two of glue on the cardboard to help hold the leaf in place and press the leaf facedown (veins facing up) onto the glue and cardboard.

4. Center a piece of foil that's slightly larger than the cardboard over the leaf.

5. Fold one side of the foil around one side of the cardboard.

6. Smooth the foil over the surface of the leaf and fold the remaining edges of foil over the cardboard. Tape the foil edges to the back of the cardboard.

7. Press down on the foil over the leaf gently with your finger. Rub your finger all over the part of foil covering the leaf. As you press down, you should begin to see the veins and edges of the leaf appearing in the foil.

8. Once you've pressed down over the whole leaf and have a complete foil print, take a permanent marker and trace around the edges of the leaf.

9. Color the leaf in with permanent marker however you'd like.

10. Use your finished artwork as a decoration around the house or give it as a gift.

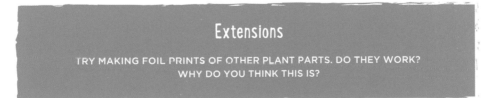

Extensions

TRY MAKING FOIL PRINTS OF OTHER PLANT PARTS. DO THEY WORK?
WHY DO YOU THINK THIS IS?

Soil Study

In a healthy environment there is so much life, even in a tiny space. In this activity we'll focus on the smaller inhabitants on the ground outside and make a guess about the health of the soil.

MATERIALS

- [ ] Ruler or measuring tape
- [ ] Shovel or hand shovel
- [ ] Notebook
- [ ] Sifter (or stapler, window screen or wire mesh, and old photo frame)

DIRECTIONS

1. If you don't have a sifter, you can often find old flour sifters at the local thrift store or you can make one using an old or inexpensive wood picture frame and window screen. To make one, remove the glass or plastic from a frame and lay the frame facedown. Cut a piece of window screen that has the same dimensions as the outside of the frame. Lay the cut window screen over the back of the frame and use a stapler to staple the screen to the frame in several places.

2. Gather the sifter, shovel, measuring tape, and notebook and choose a patch of grass to explore.

3. Measure a square foot of land—a square with 12-inch (1-foot) sides.

4. Inspect the top layer of the square. What do you see? Do you see living plants or animals? What kind? Record what you find in your notebook.

5. Dig into the square and look at what you see. Do you see roots? Dead plants? Any creatures?

6. Scoop a few scoops of dirt onto the sifter and sift. What's left behind? Did you discover any living creatures or larvae using the sifter? What do you think they are?

7. When scientists investigate the health of soil, they look at many different things. One of the things they look at is whether there are earthworms! If you found earthworms, chances are the soil is fairly healthy. Earthworms can only live in soil with the correct amount of plant material and nutrients, a healthy amount of moisture, and a good temperature. If you didn't see any earthworms, it could just be that the soil is too dry. Try checking back on a rainy day and see if you find any.

8. Another good way to tell if you have healthy soil is to count the number of different living things you find. The more living plants and creatures, the more likely the soil is healthy.

Extensions

REVISIT THIS SAME SQUARE FOOT OF LAND IN EACH SEASON. HOW DOES WHAT YOU FIND VARY BY SEASON?

REVISIT THIS SAME SQUARE FOOT OF LAND WHEN IT IS RAINING OUTSIDE. HOW DOES THIS CHANGE WHAT YOU FIND?

Mud Pies

There are few things in nature as fun as mud—it's messy and sensory rich! If there isn't a good dirt patch nearby, grab a bag of top soil from the local gardening store and head out to the backyard for some muddy-licious cooking! We love to scavenge our local thrift store for interesting cooking supplies for our makeshift mud kitchen, but clean containers from your recycling bin work just as well!

MATERIALS

☐ Containers   ☐ Dirt   ☐ Water   ☐ Natural objects

DIRECTIONS

1. Mix just enough water into the dirt to make it moldable.
2. Create as many delicious pretend treats as you want. Cakes and cupcakes are our favorites.
3. Decorate your creations.

BONUS ACTIVITY

Make mud body paint by mixing just enough water into dirt that it has the consistency of tempera paint. Use your fingers or a paintbrush to make interesting designs on your arms, legs, and feet!

Nature Journal

A nature journal is a great way to record thoughts or observations when you are out in nature. To study nature like a scientist, use the journal to make sketches of what you see or to record numbers or measurements. You might also use the nature journal to record collected treasures or to write down thoughts. If you love writing, use it to write poems or songs about what you see or how nature makes you feel. No matter how you use it, a nature journal is a handy thing to have during nature explorations.

MATERIALS

- ☐ Paper
- ☐ Hole punch
- ☐ Decorated cover art (optional)
- ☐ Rubber band
- ☐ Stick

DIRECTIONS

1. If you'd like to use a piece of artwork for the cover, grab that.
2. Take several pieces of white paper and fold them in half. If there is a specific cover you'd like to use, fold that in half on the outside of the papers.
3. Along the binding of the stack of papers, use a hole punch to punch one hole about 2 inches from the top and 1 inch from the edge and a second hole about 2 inches from the bottom and 1 inch from the edge.
4. Find a stick or twig and snap it so it is approximately as tall as the journal.
5. Loop a rubber band over the top edge of the stick, pull the rubber band tightly against the stick, and thread the rest of the rubber band through the top hole on the front of the journal toward the back.
6. Reach behind the journal and pull the rubber band down through the second hole to make a rubber band loop that comes out toward the front of the journal.
7. Stretch the rubber band loop out and over the bottom of the stick to secure it.
8. You should now be able to open the journal to write or draw what you'd like. The rubber band and stick should hold the paper together and serve as the binding of the journal.

Extensions

WRITE POEMS OR STORIES IN YOUR NATURE JOURNAL ABOUT WHAT YOU SEE.

SKETCH INTERESTING THINGS YOU FIND OUTSIDE.

Flower Press

Pressing flowers and leaves is a great way to preserve samples and to create supplies for future art projects! There are many ways to press flowers and leaves, but here we'll share two of our favorites. If you love the flower press, remember that it can also make a great gift for a friend.

MATERIALS

Option A

- [ ] Cardboard
- [ ] Rubber bands
- [ ] White paper
- [ ] Scissors
- [ ] Flowers or leaves

Option B

- [ ] Two pieces of sanded wood that are cut to the same size
- [ ] Cardboard
- [ ] Scissors
- [ ] Tall screws
- [ ] Washers (that fit the screws)
- [ ] Drill
- [ ] Wing nuts (that fit the screws)
- [ ] Flowers or leaves

DIRECTIONS

Option A:

1. To make a simple flower press, cut five pieces of cardboard that are approximately 8 inches long by 4 inches wide.

2. Cut eight pieces of white paper that are approximately 8 inches long by 4 inches wide.

3. Set one piece of cardboard down, cover it with a piece of white paper, and place flowers or leaves on the paper so they do not overlap or hang off the edge. Cover them with a layer of white paper, and then repeat until you've placed the last piece of paper and cardboard.

4. Wrap 3 to 5 rubber bands tightly around the press so that they are evenly spaced along the length of the cardboard.

5. Leave the press for 1 to 2 weeks or longer.

6. Remove the rubber bands and gently remove the paper and cardboard layers. An adult may need to delicately remove some flowers so they don't get damaged.

Option B:

1. Cut two pieces of wood (any size) so that they have the same dimensions. Sand them to remove any splinters or to smooth rough edges.

2. Ask an adult to drill holes that are spaced every 4 to 6 inches along the outside of the wood pieces. Take care to drill the holes about 1 inch in from the edge of the wood. The holes should go through both pieces of wood. Sand the drilled holes to remove any splinters or to smooth rough edges.

3. Use one piece of the wood to measure a cardboard template. The cardboard should have the same shape as the wood, but smaller dimensions so it fits on the inside portion between the holes and does not cover them.

4. Use the cardboard template to cut cardboard pieces (7 is a good number to start with).

5. Use the cardboard template to cut white paper pieces (12 is a good number to start with).

6. Thread the screws through one of the pieces of wood so that the head of the screw is flat on the ground (along with the wood) and the body of the screw sticks up.

7. Place a cardboard piece in the center of the wood such that it nestles between the screws.

8. Place a white sheet of paper down and place flowers or leaves on the paper so they do not overlap or hang off the edge. Cover them with a layer of white paper.

9. Repeat steps 7 and 8 until you've placed the last piece of paper and cardboard.

10. Thread the top piece of wood onto the screws.

11. Place a washer on each screw and a wing nut on each washer, and then tighten them.

12. Depending on the cut of the wood, it's possible to tighten too much and cause stress fractures in the wood. Aim to tighten enough that the cardboard is compressed, but not so much that you strain the wood.

Extensions

MAKE YOUR OWN NATURE GUIDE BY LABELING THE PRESSED VERSIONS OF DIFFERENT LOCAL PLANTS AND FLOWERS WITH THEIR NAMES.

BONUS ACTIVITY

Buy clear glass decorative gems and small magnets at a craft store. Paint a thin layer of glue on the flat back of the gems and gently press a flower, facedown, into the glue. Paint a second thin layer of glue over the flower and allow to dry. Once dry, use hot glue or super glue to attach a small magnet. Decorate the refrigerator or with the flower magnets.

Nature Paintbrushes

No paintbrush? No problem! Make your own! What sorts of natural materials make the sturdiest paintbrushes? Which type of natural material makes the prettiest pattern when you paint with it?

MATERIALS

☐ Several short sticks ☐ Rubber bands ☐ Watercolor paint ☐ Paper
☐ Different types of leaves, grasses, mosses, and other natural materials

DIRECTIONS

1. Gather the materials and choose what to use to make your first paintbrush.

2. Attach the materials to the end of one stick with a rubber band.

3. Decide if you want to leave the material as is, or trim it to fit, or cut it to see if the cuts you make leave behind patterns.

4. Repeat steps 2 through 3 to make as many paintbrushes as you'd like.

5. Fill cups with a small amount of liquid watercolors or other paint.

6. Dip the paintbrush and experiment with paint strokes. What pattern does it leave behind when you barely brush it against the paper? What about when you press down hard?

7. Create art using all of the paintbrushes.

8. Which types of paintbrushes lasted for the whole paint session? Did you have any paintbrushes that broke or fell apart? Why do you think this is?

9. Which paintbrushes left the most interesting patterns? Why do you think this is?

10. If you were going to do this activity again, would you use different materials to make the paintbrushes? Why?

BONUS ACTIVITY

Find a large leaf (or several large leaves). Paint the back of the leaf with a thin layer of paint. Press it down firmly on a piece of paper and smooth it out with your hands. Gently peel the leaf back to reveal a beautiful print. Can you think of anything else you could use as a nature stamp? Try it out and see what sort of print it leaves behind!

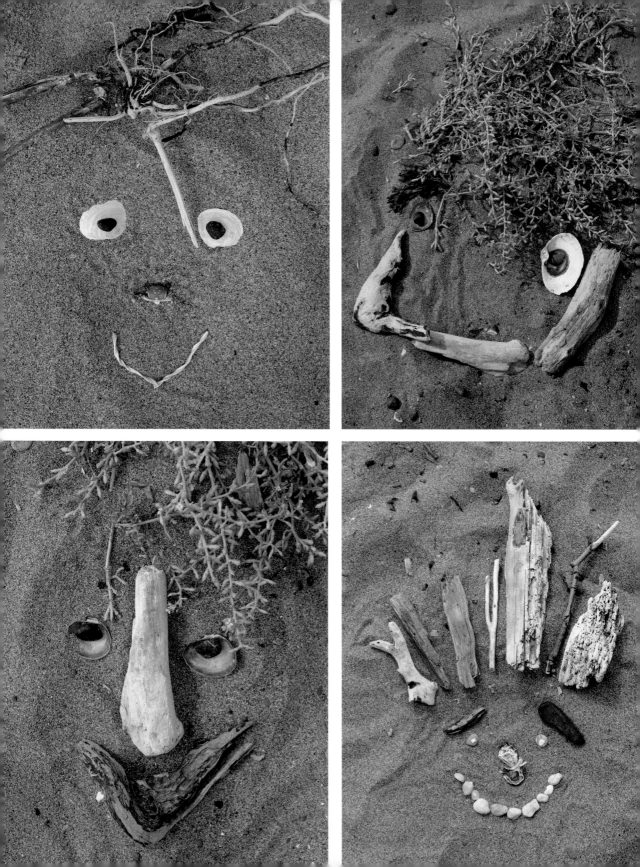

Nature Faces

Can you use the different shapes and colors in nature to make a face? Go on a hunt for nature hair, eyes, ears, and noses and see what you can create.

MATERIALS

☐ Natural objects   ☐ Camera (optional)

DIRECTIONS

1. Find a flat space that's sheltered from wind.
2. Go search for objects you could use for eyes, ears, mouth, nose, hair, and any other parts of a face that you'd like to add.
3. Can you make a happy face? Sad face? What about angry?
4. Can you make the side of a face?
5. Can you make an entire person?

Extensions

CAN YOU MAKE A SCENE FOR A STORY USING NATURAL OBJECTS? CAN YOU TELL A STORY USING THAT SCENE?

CHECK OUT A BOOK OR DO AN INTERNET SEARCH ABOUT THE WORK OF ANDY GOLDSWORTHY. CAN YOU THINK OF OTHER THINGS YOU'D LIKE TO TRY TO MAKE USING NATURAL OBJECTS?

Leaf Luminaries

With the early darkness of fall (and if you experience power outages during fall or winter storms), it might be nice to have additional lighting. This craft is a fun way to bring nature's beauty inside your home. We show fall leaves here, but you could repeat this with any season!

MATERIALS

☐ Empty clear plastic or glass jars (clean and dry, and with an opening wide enough to fit an LED tea light)

☐ Glue   ☐ Paintbrush   ☐ Pressed fall leaves   ☐ LED tea lights

DIRECTIONS

1. Gather fall leaves and press them between papers inside a heavy book or press them using a Flower Press (page 110) for at least a week prior to starting this project.

2. Collect clear glass or plastic bottles with wide openings from your recycling bin.

3. Place glue in a dish and use a paintbrush to brush a coat of glue all over the container.

4. Press and smooth the pressed leaves onto the glue-covered surface of the bottle.

5. Once you have placed the leaves on the bottle, paint one more coat of glue over both the leaves and the bottle.

6. Allow the bottle to dry overnight.

7. Place an LED tea light in the center of the luminary and enjoy!

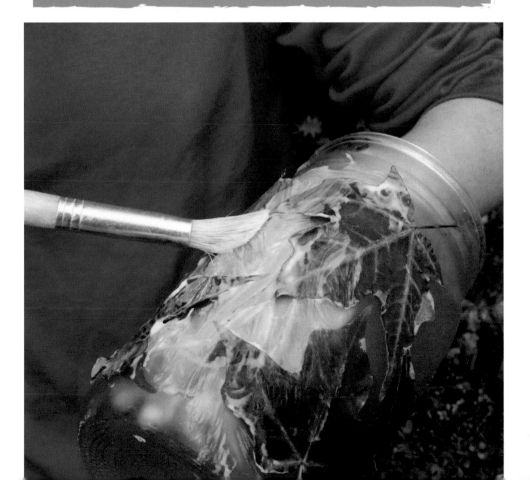

Negative Space Art

We often make art by coloring inside spaces, so sometimes it's hard to remember that we can color around something! Creating a picture by coloring the space outside something is called negative space art. There are many ways to do it—by using paint or chalk or markers. One of our favorite ways to make it is by using a spray bottle.

MATERIALS

☐ Spray bottle ☐ Liquid watercolors ☐ Natural objects ☐ Paper

DIRECTIONS

1. Place the objects on the paper. Flatter objects will leave more distinct prints. If you'd like to get detailed leaf prints, I suggest placing them facedown.

2. Either attach a sprayer from a spray bottle to the bottle of liquid watercolors or pour a small amount of liquid watercolor in the bottom of a spray bottle. For the best results, do not dilute the watercolors.

3. Spray a pattern all over the painting (on the natural objects and around them).

4. Repeat steps 2 and 3 for as many different watercolor paints as you'd like.

5. Allow the painting to dry.

6. Remove the natural objects to reveal the prints!

7. As an alternative to using watercolors and a spray bottle, you can hold the objects in place with one hand and paint with tempera paint around them. You can also arrange objects on a driveway or sidewalk and spray them with water to make temporary negative space art!

BONUS ACTIVITY

Make mysterious leaf prints by placing leaves facedown on a flat surface and covering them with white paper. Using the side of a peeled white crayon, press down firmly and color over the leaves. Once you've colored over the entire leaf (or all the leaves) with the white crayon thoroughly, get a paintbrush and watercolors. Paint over the white crayon-colored side of the paper. The leaf outlines should magically appear as the white crayon resists the watercolor. You can use the same initial technique to make crayon rubbings of leaves with lots of different crayon colors.

Nature Treasure Collections

We often take vacations in or near state or national parks. Our kids love to search the forest floor and beaches for treasures, but it is illegal to remove these objects from a protected space such as these parks. Instead we collect fallen objects and then arrange them and take a picture of our treasures. These treasure collections are still a fun exercise, even if you don't get to take the physical treasures with you, and they are a unique way to document the special natural spaces we visit.

MATERIALS

- [ ] Natural objects
- [ ] Camera

DIRECTIONS

1. Gather up any interesting treasures you find on a hike, walk, or beach trip.
2. Arrange them how you wish.
3. Take a photo and leave the objects behind.

Extensions

USE A NATURE HANDBOOK OR INTERNET SEARCH TO IDENTIFY SOME OR ALL OF THE OBJECTS IN YOUR COLLECTION. WHAT ARE THEY NAMED? ARE THEY NATIVE OR INVASIVE? ARE THEY COMMON OR RARE?

Appendix A

Resources

RESOURCES MENTIONED IN THE BOOK

SURF YOUR WATERSHED

Visit the US Environmental Protection Agency's website and enter your US address to find what watershed you belong to. This also includes the names and contacts of any organizations that work on improving and monitoring the water quality in your watershed.

cfpub.epa.gov/surf/locate/index.cfm

BUILD A BIRDHOUSE

Visit the Sialis website to learn what the ideal nestbox dimensions are for your local bird species.

www.sialis.org/nestboxguide.htm

MAKE A PHOTO COLLAGE FOR FREE

Visit the Picmonkey website and click on "Collage" from the homepage. Select the photos you'd like to use from your computer and use the options on the left to create your collage.

www.picmonkey.com

ADDITIONAL RESOURCES

Craftiments
www.craftiments.com

Buggy and Buddy
www.buggyandbuddy.com

My Nearest and Dearest
www.mynearestanddearest.com

Messy Little Monster
www.messylittlemonster.com

The Inspired Treehouse
www.theinspiredtreehouse.com

Teach Preschool
www.teachpreschool.org

INSPIRING NATURE AUTHORS TO CHECK OUT

Claire Walker Leslie   Stacy Tornio   Jo Schofield and Fiona Danks

Dawn Isaac   Erin Kenny   Richard Louv

Lynn Brunelle   Scott Sampson   Helen Ross Russell

Macroinvertebrate Identification Chart

Group A: These macroinvertebrates are very sensitive to pollution. You will only find them in clean water.

caddisfly   mayfly   stonefly

Group B: These macroinvertebrates are sensitive to pollution. You will find them in clean water and water with only a small amount of pollution.

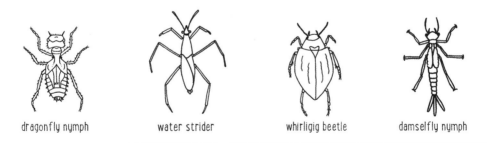

dragonfly nymph   water strider   whirligig beetle   damselfly nymph

Group C: These macroinvertebrates are very tollerant of pollution. You will find them in almost any kind of water, including heavily polluted water.

boatman   mosquito larvae   freshwater snail   leech

Index

About the Author

Asia Citro has an MEd in Science Education and was a classroom science teacher for many years before deciding to stay home full time after the birth of her daughter. She lives near Seattle with her wonderful husband, two awesome children, and two destructive cats. She started her blog *Fun at Home with Kids* in February 2013 and has since spent many late nights experimenting with new play recipes, sensory materials, science experiments, and art projects. Her first book, *150+ Screen-Free Activities for Kids*, was published in November 2014 and her second book, *The Curious Kid's Science Book*, was published in September 2015. To read about her most recent late-night discoveries or to see more photos of her adorable kids at play, visit www.funathomewithkids.com.